'A wonderfully written, honest
prophets and prayer. In her c
Debbie walks us into the world of the p...
our daily living. I loved this book; it gave me so much to feed
on and take away. So good!'

*Revd Cris Rogers, All Hallows Church, Bow*

'The Minor Prophets rarely rate among our hot favourite Bible
books, yet Debbie Duncan encourages us to take a journey of
discovery. *Minor Prophets, Major Prayer* is a useful reference
tool for personal study, full of enlightening biblical history that
sets both author and message in context, allowing the reader
to move from 'What did it say then?' to 'What does it mean
for me today . . . especially for my prayer life?' There's nothing
'minor' about this book. Between the covers you'll grapple with
life's big issues: a God you cannot ignore; a commitment you
need to make; a prayer life you can experience.'

*Catherine Campbell, author*

'I am so glad Debbie wrote this book. In it I have discovered
hidden treasure in books of the Bible I wished I had studied
more. Insights that have challenged my thinking, encouragements that have kept me going and inspiration to keep believing. Highly recommended.'

*Patrick Regan OBE, founder of Kintsugi Hope*

'As we grapple with how to live life to the full in this Covid-19
pandemic; the wisdom, honesty and reality of the prayer life
of the Minor Prophets has much to teach us. This timely book

helps to reframe our perceptions of the God to whom we pray and inspires us to journey on with the One who never fails or forsakes us.'

*Jane Holloway, World Prayer Centre, Birmingham*

'I must confess that as I started reading *Minor Prophets, Major Prayers* I felt a niggle of embarrassment as I realised that, despite my several decades of being a Christian and in full-time ministry, I've mostly skimmed quickly through the minor prophets rather than taking the time to study them in depth. I've always felt rather alienated by their predominant themes of sin and judgment and have quickly moved onto other favourite passages. But in this lovely book, Debbie and other contributing authors gently bring alive the history and heart of each individual prophet in a way that is rich and eye-opening. A wealth of both scriptural and cultural information is given in a wholly readable and engageable way. You find yourself taken up with the political and moral conflicts of the time and suddenly realising not just how applicable they are to our present day, but also to our own lives. Through these pages I've encountered the God of incredible patience, faithfulness, compassion and love and heard His heart longing that we live our lives with Him at the centre, knowing Him, loving Him and letting our heart passions be united with His. As Debbie explores each prophet, so my own response to issues like injustice and hypocrisy or my own battles with idolatry and sidelining of God are revealed so it becomes a tool of self-revelation and change as well as teaching and understanding – a wonderful achievement! I am delighted to recommend this book to all.'

*Tracy Williamson, author, co-leader MBM Trust*

'Debbie has a remarkable way of bringing the minor prophets to life, books I had previously avoided. We are taken on a fascinating journey through historical events of God's people. There are lessons to be learned. God will not overlook sin but is patient and loving, giving His people many opportunities to turn back to Him. This is a challenging reminder to me of the importance of prayer and to be continually in repentance before God. A clear and concise book which I will refer back to many times.'

*Sharon Bailie, follower of Jesus, loves the Bible*

'This lovely book by Debbie Duncan provides helpful insight into the Minor Prophets, and encourages us to respond to their messages in prayer. Practical and thought-provoking, this book is a great tool for discipleship.'

*Matthew Porter, Vicar of The Belfry,*
*York and author*

# Minor Prophets, Major Prayer

## Getting real with God

Debbie Duncan

Authentic

First published 2021 by Authentic Media Limited,
PO Box 6326, Bletchley, Milton Keynes, MK1 9GG.
authenticmedia.co.uk

**British Library Cataloguing in Publication Data**
A catalogue record for this book is available from the British Library.
ISBN: 978-1-78893-121-2
978-1-78893-122-9 (e-book)

Cover design by Danc
Printed and bound by CPI Group (UK) Ltd, Croydon, CR0 4YY

# Contents

## Contents

This book is dedicated to those people that have taught me so much about prayer. They are warriors and some are saints – I salute them.

For my remarkable husband, Malcolm – you are my constant companion on this journey. Thank you. And to my family: Matthew and Eve, Benjamin, Ellie and Arthur, Anna, Jacob and Caleb, and Riodhna. You are all extraordinary.

I also want to dedicate this book to my family at Dundonald Elim Church. You have welcomed us and loved us. What more can I say? We feel part of the family. I thank God we are on this journey together.

# Acknowledgments

I love completing a manuscript knowing I must write my thank yous. I have a lot!

Thank you to Malcolm. I am so grateful that you are my closest companion – one that I can praise and lament with. I love you more than ever, even though you are 50!

Thank you to my wonderful family who love me, pray for me and listen to me as I go over what I am studying. You really are extraordinary, and I am so proud to be your mum. Thank you to Matthew and Eve, Benjamin, Ellie and Arthur, Anna and Jacob and Caleb and Riodhna. To Rob and Emily: I am so grateful for our ever-growing family.

Thank you to my wonderful daughter, Anna Arnold, and her insightful chapter on Amos. I love your heart. Thank you, too, to Cathy Le Feuvre – isn't it wonderful to write together again.

Thank you to my first family at Authentic Media who published my first book *Life Lines* which I co-authored with Cathy Le Feuvre in 2014. Thank you to Donna Harris who welcomed me back.

**Author information:**

Anna Arnold has from a young age been fascinated with justice, which led her down a legal career route. After studying law in Belfast, she located there with her husband, Jacob. She now works in a local law firm and hopes to become an asylum and immigration barrister. She also loves singing and writing.

Cathy Le Feuvre is an author and broadcaster based in Jersey in the Channel Islands. Among her books are several about the history and the founders of The Salvation Army, which is her church of choice. Cathy first collaborated and laughed a lot with Debbie Duncan on *Life Lines* (Authentic: 2014), a fun book featuring the life and times of two fictional Christian women. She currently works as a producer/presenter at BBC Radio Jersey where she specialises in faith and community stories and projects. Find out more about Cathy at www. cathylefeuvre.com.

# Foreword

We live in uncertain times. Since the beginning of 2020, the world has tried to navigate its way along the most precarious of paths. On one side the impact of a pandemic, on the other the uncertainty of our politics. In the United States of America there are continued conflicts around race, culture and the direction of the country. In the United Kingdom and the rest of Europe, we continue to try to work out what it looks like to live in a 'Post-Brexit' world. All of these big challenges touch down in the lives of ordinary women and men. How do we earn a living? What do we do to offer security and safety to our families? How do we keep our heads above water? How do we not just survive but find a way of thriving in the midst of so much change? At the heart of the answers to such questions, at least from a Christian perspective, sits the possibilities availed to us through prayer.

When God's people face uncertain times, they pray. When they do not know what to do, they pray. When they want to remain faithful, they pray. When they are surrounded by opposition, the unknown or challenges that need to be navigated, they pray. We are called to this most remarkable of endeavours by God in every aspect of our lives. Our Creator invites us into dialogue and intimate relationship with Godself. It is, perhaps, regrettable that so many followers of Christ see prayer as a last resort or as a practise that we employ to get us through a tight spot or a profound challenge, when actually prayer is to be, in the words of the old hymn 'the Christian's vital breath'. To pray is to be reminded that we are in need, that we are not the centre of the universe, and that there is hope. The act of praying is, in itself, an acknowledgment that the answers to the dilemmas we face lie beyond ourselves. It is an implicit confession that we need the help of Another if we are to navigate the world around us. It is also a quest for answers to the questions that we are confronted by in the world around us. Why is the world the way it is? What can we do to fix it? Where do we find hope that can sustain us through the journey?

The call to pray, to seek God, to listen for God's Voice, is as old as the very Story of God. From the mysterious picture of God communing with Adam and Eve in the Garden of Eden in the opening pages of the Bible to the closing words of the New Testament in which we are called to commune with God and to walk with God in the new Garden City where death, sorrow and pain will be no more, we are continually invited into dialogue and conversation with the Sustainer of all things. Such conversation is more than pietistic petitions seeking personal blessing, though. It would seem that God's idea of prayer often seems very different from what we have turned prayer into. The prayers of Scripture can rage at God, question the events that surround God's people and wrestle with issues of pain, sorrow, suffering and loss. I am not sure we really know how to pray? As a pastor, I wonder what many Christians would do if they heard someone pray as Moses or Abraham did, when they seem to bargain with God for Israel? The desperation of David, the despair of Jeremiah and the peculiar and outlandish behaviour of characters such as Isaiah and Ezekiel would leave many modern pilgrims scratching their head in wonder and shuffling away from these unusual praying people to keep a respectable distance. Hannah's heartfelt brokenness and desperation, when overheard by another, were interpreted as the mumblings of a foolish drunken woman, when actually they were probably some of the most abandoned cries a human can utter. To truly pray, it would seem, is to be undone in God's presence, and to enter a place of petition, yearning, and ultimately revelation and discovery that can turn your world the right way up again and alter your perspective on how things should be forever. If ever there was a time to dig more deeply into this ancient rite and to practice this life-sustaining discipline, it is now. Anything that can help us do this must surely be welcome.

This book helps us to rediscover the deep riches that can be mined as we explore the prayer lives and the heart cries of the prophets of Ancient Israel. They offer us a way of praying and communing with God that stands in danger of being lost amidst the cultural clutter of our very modern world. They remind us that prayer addresses issues of justice, poverty, freedom, human rights, treatment of the poor and profound human yearning. These are the prayers that have shaped cultures and changed the world. It is, for example, a surprise to many Americans that Martin Luther King did not originate the phrase 'Let justice flow like rivers and righteousness as a never-ending stream'. King's vision of a fairer, better America was rooted in Amos's sense of God's desire for a fairer, better Israel and world. There is much that we can discover about the purpose, power and principles of prayer from the prophets of Israel. They teach us how to think more broadly than ourselves, how to listen for the voice of God, not just into our own lives but also into our churches, our communities and our societies. They help us catch a clearer glimpse of what it means to live faithfully, to serve wholeheartedly and to live purposefully.

Debbie's book helps us to re-discover these ancient ways. She skilfully excavates the treasures to be found in the prophets, furnishing us with freshly discovered metaphors, pictures and principles of prayer. She broadens our horizons to see that praying with the prophets involves seeing that we face many of the same issues as they did. Just like them, we live in a world where followers of Yahweh can be too selfish. Just like them, we are confronted with our narrowing of God's great purposes to our own ends. Just like them, we need to be reminded that justice matters, not just us. Just like them, we have to wrestle with how we approach materialism, hedonism and experientialism. Just like them, we must leave the spiritual jacuzzies of what God can do for us and enter the worlds of the broken, the forgotten and the disenfranchised if we are ever to discover the depths of possibility for change and hope that lie in the heart of God.

I commend this book, not because it is written by my wife, but because it is an important book. It is a call to remember that despite the challenges we face and the uncertainties that surround us, there is a way of hope for all of us to walk. In the end, it is not that complicated. We, like the audience who first heard Micah, are reminded that God requires three simple things of us – to act justly, love mercy and walk humbly with the One who created us and who flung stars into space.

Our world will not be changed by politicians, educationalists, or social entrepreneurs on their own. Medical and technological advances in and of themselves are not enough. We will not see societies transformed, communities brought together and the deep divisions of our world overcome by simply trying harder. We need God. When Aleksandr Solzhenitsyn accepted the Templeton Prize in the early 1980s, he used his acceptance speech to remind his audience and the wider world that at the heart of the challenges faced by the Soviet Union was the reality that people had forgotten God. He reminded them that the line between good and evil passes between every human heart.

The challenges that our world is confronted with are not answered by the 'left' or the 'right'. They cannot be divided up into a set of people with the right political answers and the wrong ones. Our world will not be better if everyone becomes an upholder of social liberal democracy. The challenges we face, the hurdles we must overcome and the devastations that surround us will not be adequately addressed by bigger budgets and better ideas. We need to learn to pray again. We need to discover that prayer changes us and then changes our communities, our cultures and ultimately our perspective on the world.

When Jesus' followers heard Him pray, they asked Him to teach them how to pray. As we read the words of this book, may we fall on our knees once again, with a better, clearer and stronger vision of God's Kingdom and God's purposes and cry with all of our hearts, 'Oh, that you would rend the heavens and come down.' For it is only as God's people cry out to God, listening for what God says and being willing to obey God's voice, that we have any hope of navigating the way ahead. Our hope lies in God alone – may this book help us see that once again and give us words that we need to express our yearning desire for God to visit us, and our world, in fresh power.

Revd Malcolm J. Duncan F.R.S.A.
County Down
October 2020

Therefore, my dear brothers and sisters,
stand firm. Let nothing move you. Always
give yourselves fully to the work of the Lord,
because you know that your labour in the
Lord is not in vain.

*1 Cor. 15:58*

# Introduction

# The Background to the Minor Prophets

As a family, in the past few years we have had some interesting challenges around loss and grief. We were never told this journey with God was going to be easy. It has in fact been full of raw emotion – of the deepest joy and peace and of deafening sorrow. During times of deep emotion, we have turned again and again to God with our petitions and prayers of lament. Sometimes we have not been able to verbalise how we feel and have but echoed the words of the psalmist or the minor prophets as we have navigated some deep valleys and high mountains. I have found solace in these places, but they are not just for times of despair. As I have journeyed through the night of grief into morning, these passages of Scripture have become more precious to me. I must confess I love the New Testament, but I have also come to love the books of the minor prophets. I love how God's plan for our redemption unrolls from Genesis, at the start of time, until Revelation. These books paint God with words such as holy, sovereign, loving, gracious and merciful.

Hosea tells us about God's passionate love for His people, Joel challenges us about complacency, Amos reminds us that God loves justice, Micah reminds us to live just and merciful lives. Zechariah tells us about hope in a hopeless time, Malachi brings us a message of hope for the future. Their words are dramatic, graphic, poetic and prophetic.

Their words have helped me as I have learned to pray.

This book pulls out the lessons from the minor prophets and asks the question, 'What do they teach us about our relationship with God? What do they teach us about prayer?'

This may not be an easy book to read. Each chapter is slightly different, just as the books are different in style and language. There are also a couple of contributors that add colour and realism to the chapters they have written. I sent the manuscript to my friend Sharon – she told me she felt it was a winter book. What she meant was that it was not a book you would read on your summer beach holiday. It is a book you would read when you have time to digest the words and ruminate on them. She laughed when she told me it was a winter book as she said it was a compliment, as living in Northern Ireland our winter can feel like quite a long time. She read it in a few days but had to pause, stop, think and go back to it. What she did tell me was that it made her think about who she prays to and how she prays. My prayer for you as you read it is that the lives and words of the minor prophets help you in your understanding of who God is. Come back to the book as often as you want. My prayer is that it will help you develop a deeper understanding of God and how to talk to Him.

I have often heard people say, 'Prayer is simply a communication process that allows us to talk to God.' I know that God really wants us to talk to Him. You'd think in this age of communication we would get what this means – that we would pray more. We live in an age where we have mobile phones, the internet, social media. When I went to Uganda for the first time in 2010, I was shocked by the number of people who had mobile phones and by the number of phone shops. Here were people struggling to get food or fresh water, but they all had a mobile phone. It was reported in 2013 that six of the world's 7 billion people have mobile phones – but only 4.5 billion have a toilet, according to a study in 2010 outlined in *The Wall Street Journal*.[1] Americans spend 63.5 billion minutes on social networks and blogs.[2] Another study highlights that an average internet user spends sixty-eight hours on the internet per month, which is just over about two hours a day.[3] If we are such good communicators, why does prayer seem such a problem? Many people think prayer is complicated. They are not sure how to pray and so just do not do it. How can we be such great communicators with each other but not with God who loves us unconditionally?

Prayer is not just communicating, though, as the Catechism defines it as 'the raising of one's mind and heart to God'.[4] Or as Thérèse of Lisieux, the Carmelite nun said, 'The surge of the heart; it is a simple look turned toward heaven, it is a cry of recognition and of love, embracing both trial and joy.'[5]

There is certainly a lot written about prayer. My husband must have thousands of books – he really has a library with a Dewey decimal system, so he knows where they are. We moved to a new house two years ago, and they are spread across two offices and bookshelves in our garage. He has a whole section of books dedicated to prayer.

There are so many different forms of prayer; it can be done privately in our secret place, or it may be done corporately in the presence of other believers. Prayer can be incorporated into our daily lives at random times as we walk around, or we may have a set time each day to pray. We may light candles, read liturgy, or fast and pray. We may even sit, stand, kneel, or lay prostrate on the floor. We may be quiet as a mouse or roar with pain and confusion. There is no set pattern to prayer, only guidance through the Scriptures and the template that Jesus gave us in the Lord's Prayer.

The main types of prayer are praise, petition or supplication, intercession and thanksgiving. Certainly, we read about these forms of prayer through the minor prophets. Read the following passages as the prophets came before God with petition or supplication, earnestly asking God to intervene for them or on behalf of their nation:

> Let us go at once to entreat the LORD and seek the LORD Almighty. I myself am going.
>
> *Zech. 8:21*

> When my life was ebbing away, I remembered you, LORD, and my prayer rose to you, to your holy temple.
>
> *Jonah 2:7*

> So I turned to the Lord God and pleaded with him in prayer and petition, in fasting, and in sackcloth and ashes. I prayed to the LORD my God and confessed: 'Lord, the great and awesome God, who keeps his covenant of love with those who love him and keep his commandments . . .
>
> *Dan. 9:3,4*

There are also intercessory prayers, much like that of petition, praying on behalf of others.

Intercession is powerful. In Hebrew it means to effect change by accident, enforced or just by importunity. Their prayers are delivered with such force as to make a violent impression. I can just see Habakkuk interceding for the people, pounding his fists on the ground, making an impression in the soil beneath him.

This powerful type of prayer is what Jesus does for us. Paul, talking about Jesus in Hebrews 7:25, says, 'Therefore he is able to save completely those who come to God through him, because he always lives to intercede for them.'

As Christians we should not underestimate the power of prayer. James 5:16 declares, 'The prayer of a righteous person is powerful and effective.' The prophets and men and women of the Bible understood the power of prayer. Why is it that we do not always pray as we should?

## We forget

Terrible, isn't it, but I think our lives can be so busy at times that we genuinely forget to pray. We get up and are in a hurry, so we decide we will talk to God later. All through the day we push our prayer slot later and later until we are suddenly in bed and too tired to pray. We decide to make more of an effort tomorrow. Perhaps that is more about how we expect to pray rather than making time to pray. Having four children under the age of 5 was certainly a challenge for me, balancing the children, work and home with a dedicated time to pray. I soon realised that I could pray anywhere and at any time. Scripture tells us to 'Devote yourselves to prayer, being watchful and thankful' (Col. 4:2). I have learned that I need to have consistent prayer rhythms in my life.

## We think it is boring

We may have had a bad experience of prayer and prayer meetings. I remember going to prayer meetings in a cold hall, tired and bored. It really put me off prayer meetings, as I thought they had to all be like it.

In 2013 the writer Jade Mazarin wrote an article on this topic for *Relevant* magazine.[6] She suggests we find prayer boring as we live in an age of instant results. We expect instant gratification, and prayer can be the opposite of that. Sometimes we can wait years for an answer, and we must be persistent at knocking at the same door. Twenty years it took for God to answer a prayer we held in our hearts. We kept asking God to change a situation. Was I bored with asking for the same thing? Of course I was! When the answer came it was so unexpected, I nearly didn't believe it. God completely changed a situation we were praying for in a way we could not imagine.

## We don't know what to say

I think sometimes we are not sure what to say. The church I went to when I first became a Christian taught me so much about God and the Bible. They did not, however, let women pray out loud in the prayer meetings. When I left home and started going to a church that had a different approach to the role of women, I used to sit in the prayer meeting unsure what to say. All the prayers I had heard out loud were male voices who used to quote passages of Scripture. My prayers were never going to sound like their prayers. Eventually, a friend told me just to talk to God out loud. I realised it was not that difficult; after all, I had been praying to Him for several years quietly in my mind. He just wanted to hear my voice.

In Romans 8:26 we are reminded that 'We do not know what we ought to pray for, but the Spirit himself intercedes for us through wordless groans'.

Not knowing what to do in prayer is one of the major reasons people do not pray. There are lots of books and plans, but I would simply say: abandon all plans, and just simply wing it by opening your mouth and saying what is on your mind to God. Prayer is like talking to your best friend. When I am on a long journey in the car with my husband, we do not talk all the time. Sometimes we have deep conversations, or we may just chat about what we see, and sometimes we sit quietly just enjoying being beside each other.

## We don't think it makes a difference

We sometimes forget the massive difference that our prayer makes. Prayer is one of the most powerful things that we can ever do. Look at the lives of these prophets, like Haggai, or Zephaniah. Prayer changed things for them.

These are some simple pointers of how to pray:

- Pray simply. You do not have to use complicated long words.
- Use the verses you read in the Bible to direct your prayers.
- Be creative – make prayer active and multi-sensory.
- Make prayer an integral part of your day.
- Learn from others.

I have been blessed to be part of a church family since I was 14 years old – that's thirty-six years! When I started going to church, the only one that seemed suitable was in our local village, which was five miles away. It was a Free Church of Scotland. If you have not been in the Highlands and Islands of Scotland, you may not know a lot about the denomination. They have around a hundred congregations all over Scotland and links to other denominations in North America, Africa, Asia and Australia. They can trace their roots to 1843 and the struggle of the Scottish Church to remain 'free' from State interference, hence their name. In a bid to be different from the State Church, congregations sat to sing and stood to pray. It may sound old-fashioned to many of us, but they had and still have a real respect and reverence of the Scripture. So, this 14-year-old girl desperate to hear about God went along most weeks to the Sunday school. There the Old and New Testaments were pieced together for me in one amazing story. I distinctly remember hearing about Jesus and how he performed the miracles of Elijah in remarkable ways. I heard about the hundred or more prophecies of Jesus in the Old Testament. I also learned about the law given on Mount Sinai and how Jesus summarised the law in Matthew 22:37–39, repeating the words of Leviticus 19:18. Each week we had to memorise a few stanzas of a psalm and a passage of Scripture. At the end of the term we even had an exam! In the church services we sang only the Psalms. I don't know many Sunday schools that would have that structure, but I am so glad that I was familiar with the psalms and the Old Testament prophets, as their words have become precious to me throughout my life.

Sometimes I must be reminded about these great truths again, especially when I find myself in difficult circumstances.

This book tells us the story of the people of God through the books of the minor prophets in the Old Testament. They may be called minor prophets, but they teach us major truths about prayer.

The chapters of this book are in chronological order and each focuses on one minor prophet from a time in Israel's history and looks at what we can learn from them. There is a section about the prophet, the background to the book, a section on the main themes and a section about how that can help us to pray.

Throughout the book we will hear the stories of how they cried out to God and He answered them. How they learned to pray with prayers of praise, petition, intercession and thanksgiving.

God met them in the situation they found themselves in. Much of what the Israelites were going through resonates with what is happening in our society today. What made them turn to God and how did they ask Him for help? My prayer is that this book will help you. Turning to Scripture often helps us to engage our hearts and mind. The passages we read pull our minds in to the challenges of life, and we find ourselves in focused prayer.

**Let's pray**

Father of creation,
Sometimes we do not know how to pray or what to say.
We know You hear our prayers – no matter what we say.
Nothing we can say will shock You.
You never turn us away.
Help us to learn to trust You, to share our lives with You.
Thank You that You listen, even though sometimes we do
    not want to hear You.
Thank You that You are always there.
Help us to learn the art of living a life of prayer.
To learn to talk with You.
In Jesus' name.
Amen.

**The story so far**

After you read this section you may feel like I sometimes do after I have eaten my Sunday dinner. All you want to do is rest and shut your eyes, as you are so full. This section is full of history – all those facts and figures that may make your eyes swim and your head hurt. To understand how the minor prophets fit into this great story, we need to reflect on what has happened so far. This means that we need to look at the history of Israel, but it will help us moving forward. Like any good story there is a beginning, a middle and an end.

The book of Genesis is our beginning and is one of the five books of Moses called the Pentateuch, meaning 'the five-fold book'. The Greek name for the book is Genesis, meaning 'origin', and it tells the stories of the creation. The Jews call the book of Genesis '*Bereshith*' which means 'in the beginning', repeating the first words of the book. The creation account of Genesis chapters 1 and 2 should make us consider who God is, who we are, what our purpose is. Genesis 3 spectacularly describes how we chose to rebel against God and how God chooses to save a world that rebels against its Creator. I was introduced to God's promise of redemption here by a wonderful godly woman, Miss Swanson, in Sunday school.

Then the LORD God said to the woman, 'What is this you have done?'

The woman said, 'The snake deceived me, and I ate.'

So the LORD God said to the snake, 'Because you have done this,

'Cursed are you above all livestock
and all wild animals!
You will crawl on your belly
and you will eat dust
all the days of your life.
And I will put enmity
between you and the woman,
and between your offspring and hers;

he will crush your head,
and you will strike his heel.'

*Gen. 3:13–15*

Genesis is generally considered to contain the history of the first 2,369 years. It is full of the stories that explain how the world around us and the human race were created.[7] In the first part of Genesis in chapters 1–11 we are given an account of creation and the history of humankind, of Adam and Eve, Cain and Abel, Noah's ark, to the time of the dispersion of the people after the Tower of Babel.

Until this point the people of the world had one language and a common speech. Together they made bricks, baking them thoroughly so they would last, and built themselves a tower reaching the heavens, not to reach God but to 'make a name for [themselves]' (Gen. 11:4). The Lord scattered them, and they stopped building the city and tower. Then in Genesis 11:10ff we hear about the line of Shem to Abram. The second part of the book gives us the early history of Israel to the death and burial of Joseph (chapters 12–50).

This book teaches us that God has a plan and that He knew what it was long before we were made.[8] God didn't suddenly think after Adam and Eve disobeyed him, 'What am I going to do with them?' He had a specific plan which is revealed throughout the Bible. We have already seen some of the details in the opening chapters of the book of Genesis. This paints the picture for us as we dig deeper into the landscape of the Old Testament. We want to know what God says to us about prayer – how we can talk to God. Understanding our relationship with Him is a good starting point.

In the later chapters of Genesis, we are introduced to Abram and Sarai, later to be called Abraham and Sarah. Some would say that the history of the Jewish people began when God made a covenant or a promise with a man called Abram.[9] He was told he would be the father of a great people if he did as God told him (Genesis 12). In fact, the apostle Paul referred to Abraham as the 'father of us all' in Romans 4:16. Genesis then ends with the death of Moses, as Joshua and the Jewish people enter the Promised Land of Canaan. They had spent forty years wandering in the wilderness until they could step into this territory. In fact, in 1444BC spies were sent to Canaan, but of the twelve spies sent in to spy on the land, only Joshua and Caleb trusted God would help them. The people did not believe God was on their side, so because of their disobedience, God told them that no one over the age of 20, except Caleb and Joshua, would enter the land. This is found in Numbers 14:30. This is the 'land flowing with milk and honey' (Exod. 3:8) that was promised to Abraham and his descendants in Genesis 15:18–21, to Isaac in Genesis 26:3 and his son Jacob in Genesis 28:13. This land extended from the river of Egypt to the Euphrates river, the boundary of which was clarified in Genesis 15:18–21. This was to be their homeland.

They entered Canaan in 1406BC, after Moses died, under Joshua's leadership. When the Israelites entered Canaan there were twelve tribes, named after the twelve sons of the patriarch Jacob who later was named Israel by God (Gen. 32:28). They were the sons of Israel and his two wives, Leah and Rachel, and two concubines, Zilpah and Bilhah.

The twelve tribes are listed in Genesis 49. This is important to know as we look at what happened to the twelve tribes.

These were:

- Reuben
- Simeon

- Levi
- Judah
- Zebulun
- Issachar
- Dan
- Gad
- Asher
- Naphtali
- Joseph
- Benjamin

Sometimes the tribe of Joseph is listed as two tribes for his sons, Ephraim and Manasseh. Jacob elevated the descendants of Ephraim and Manasseh to full tribes as they were the sons of Joseph and his Egyptian wife, Asenath. The twelve tribes became known as the nation of Israel, although each had its own unique characteristics. An example is the priestly tribe of Levi that became the Levites, the spiritual leaders of the nation.

Originally the Jewish nation prospered as a united nation under one God. At Mount Sinai, God had told Moses that if His people followed Him, they would be 'a kingdom of priests and a holy nation' (Exod. 19:6). Their leader was initially Moses, who passes the baton of leadership to Joshua and onwards. In its early days, the nation of Israel was led by judges and prophets such as Joshua (1300–1250BC) or Deborah (1250–1025BC). Samuel appointed his sons to lead Israel, but they turned from God and did not follow His ways. The people called for a king.

1 Samuel 8:1–9 tells us what happened:

When Samuel grew old, he appointed his sons as Israel's leaders. The name of his firstborn was Joel and the name of his second was Abijah, and they served at Beersheba. But his sons did not follow his ways. They turned aside after dishonest gain and accepted bribes and perverted justice.

So all the elders of Israel gathered together and came to Samuel at Ramah. They said to him, 'You are old, and your sons do not follow your ways; now appoint a king to lead us, such as all the other nations have.'

But when they said, 'Give us a king to lead us,' this displeased Samuel; so he prayed to the LORD. And the LORD told him: 'Listen to all that the people are saying to you; it is not you they have rejected, but they have rejected me as their king. As they have done from the day I brought them up out of Egypt until this day, forsaking me and serving other gods, so they are doing to you. Now listen to them; but warn them solemnly and let them know what the king who will reign over them will claim as his rights.'

In 1050BC Saul was anointed by Samuel to take the throne. In Genesis 49:10 we are reminded that Jacob blessed his son Judah, telling him that kings of Israel would be from his family line. In 1 Samuel 31:3–6 we learn that Saul died in a battle against the Philistines at Mount Gilboa, falling on his sword and dying where nearly all his sons and relations fell. The succession to his throne was contested by Ish-Bosheth who was his only son left alive, but only reigned for two years.

In 1010BC, David became king of Judah. Eventually David, Saul's son-in-law from the tribe of Judah, became king of all Israel, uniting Israel again in 1003BC. The prophet Nathan prophesied to King David. He promised that the kingship would forever remain within his descendants in 2 Samuel 7:11b–16:

The LORD declares to you that the LORD himself will establish a house for you: when your days are over and you rest with your ancestors, I will raise up your offspring to succeed you, your own flesh and blood, and I will establish his kingdom. He is the one who will build a house for my Name, and I will establish the throne of his kingdom for ever. I will be his father, and he shall be my son. When he does wrong, I will punish him with a rod wielded by men, with floggings inflicted by human hands. But my love will never be taken away from him, as I took it away from Saul, whom I removed from before you. Your house and your kingdom shall endure for ever before me; your throne shall be established for ever.

During David and his son Solomon's reign, Israel was one nation under one king. After Solomon's death, however, in 930BC, as a punishment for sins that were committed during his reign, his son Rehoboam ruled over only part of the nation. The kingdom was to be divided into two separate kingdoms. These two kingdoms were the kingdom of Judah and the house of David, whose capital was Jerusalem. Only the members of the tribes of Judah and Benjamin remained faithful to their king. The other ten tribes rebelled against Rehoboam shortly after the death of Solomon, and appointed Jeroboam, a former officer of King Solomon's, as their king. The Jewish nation was divided into the kingdom of Judah and the kingdom of Israel.

Israel, or the northern kingdom, consisted of the ten tribes of Reuben, Simeon, Zebulun, Issachar, Dan, Gad, Asher, Naphtali, Joseph (Ephraim and Manasseh). Their capital was Samaria. Jeroboam, the first king of Israel, knew Jewish people would want to visit the Holy Temple and Jerusalem, which was in the kingdom of Judah. To stop them making their pilgrimages to Jerusalem for the Jewish festivals, he erected his own temples for idol worship.[10] It was the start of their downfall, as the kingdom of Israel only existed roughly from 930BC until 720BC, when it was conquered by the Neo-Assyrian Empire.

The tribes of Benjamin and Judah (known as the kingdom of Judah or the Southern Kingdom) prospered until the defeat of the Assyrians by the Dynasty of Egypt and Neo-Babylonians trying to control the Eastern Mediterranean in 597 and 582BC.

We can learn a lot about a nation that turned from God during times of plenty and asked for his help when times were hard.[11] God spoke during those times through the minor prophets. These are twelve books, from Amos through to Zephaniah, that share with us their story of repentance, which leads to the redemption and restoration of God's people. They predicted the Assyrian takeover, the capture of Jerusalem and the Babylonian Capture. They also prophesied the promise of a return to Jerusalem and the coming Messiah. Their words are challenging, and they still challenge us today to call out to God again for His mercy.

The prophetic books were certainly of great importance to the New Testament church as they learned to listen to God and prayed for His help. They fuelled their prayers, providing them with images of the suffering servant in Isaiah 52 and 53 and pictures of the end times in Daniel. They helped them to understand God's great plan, reminding God's people of His power and compassion. Stephen reminds us of this in Acts 7.

The prophets are also very different, teaching us many things. The theologian Gary V. Smith, in his book *Interpreting the Prophetic Books*, suggests that there are three main types of prophecy.[12] Some of the prophets spoke words of God's plans for the present or immediate future, others focused on the distant future, such as warning of the captivity or the fall of Jerusalem. The third type of prophecy captures the dramatic events that will occur at the end of the world.

The prophecies describing present events are considered as narrative prophecies that give us insight into the life of the prophet and the culture at that time. They reveal how God spoke and what His words were to His people. An example is in the book of Ezekiel in chapter 3 when God gave Ezekiel words for him to digest about what would happen to the Israelites in the future. Another type of narrative is when the prophet told the people what happened in the past and what would happen in the future. An example is in Jonah, when he must speak to the people of Nineveh. Other narrative prophecies are also considered poetic, such as in Joel chapter 1.

Prophecies about a future era reveal part of God's full plan of how He would judge the wicked and reveal something of the kingdom of God. An example is in Zephaniah 3:15:

> The LORD has taken away your punishment, he has turned back your enemy. The LORD, the King of Israel, is with you; never again will you fear any harm.

The apocalyptic prophecies are sometimes hard to understand. They are like the words of Revelation, giving us an insight into a future hope. Look at some of the prophecies in the book of Daniel.

These types of prophecy also differ in speech. Hebrews 1:1 says:

> In the past God spoke to our ancestors through the prophets at many times and in various ways . . .

Smith suggests that these are called 'Genres'. These range from judgment speech, covenant speech, woe or salvation oracles or even law-suit speech.[13] The language of the prophecies is considered similar to that of Hebrew law.[14] It is good to remind ourselves that many of the genres of the Old Testament mirror that of oral tradition rather than written words. I would simply ask that you consider all these things and ask yourself, 'What are these words teaching me?'

Seventeen of the prophets wrote books that are included in our Bibles. Certainly not all the prophets wrote books, such as Elisha and Elijah. The church leader and author Colin Sinclair suggests that these books forth tell and foretell.[15] He suggests that all the prophets spoke into their specific periods, for the immediate application by the people at that time, but they also announced another future.

The last twelve books of the Old Testament may be called the 'minor prophets' but they are not of minor importance. Each chapter of this book tells us a story of one of the minor prophets and how they spoke into Israel's situation. Their words resonate with us today as we reflect on our own communities and country. We are taught so much about prayer throughout the Bible:

- To pray in faith (Jas 1:6).
- To address God our Father (Matt. 6:9).
- To pray in Jesus' name (John 14:13).
- To offer prayers in reverence and humility (Luke 18:13).
- To keep going (Luke 18:1).
- To submit to God and His will (Matt. 6:10).
- We are to pour out our soul to the Lord (1 Sam. 1:15).
- To cry out to heaven (2 Chr. 32:20).
- To kneel before the Father (Eph. 3:14).

The minor prophets have a lot to teach us about it as we learn about their journey and as we hear about how they were caught up in huge political upheavals, coping with their cities being besieged and eventually being taken to Babylon. They had seventy years of uncertainty, wondering why God had forgotten them. Their prayers can fill our open hands as we begin to understand that some of their challenges are remarkably like ours.

As I write this book at the start of 2020, as a country we are planning to exit the European Union, our political parties are in a mess, and President Trump has been impeached and wants to buy Greenland from Denmark. There are swarms of locusts chomping their way through Africa and we are carefully monitoring the outbreak of Covid-19. All this uncertainty blocks our vision. The words of the minor prophets can speak into our situation today. Their lament over Israel can become our own lament. This is the raw material of prayer.

**Prayer**

Father God,
I feel like I am standing in the centre of a storm and the world is whizzing around us. It is frightening, scary and I feel that all I can do is shout for help.
Help me to keep my eyes focused on You. You are the giver of life. You hold the world in your hands and keep the world spinning on its right axis.
Remind us that You are in control.
Remind us that nothing is a surprise to You.
Remind us that You are with us in the storm.
Remind us that we can trust in You.
In Jesus' name.
Amen

# 1
## Jonah

# When Things Don't Go Our Way

It was the first 'weekend away' I had ever been on with a group of Christians. I was 18 years old. I had been on a youth camp, but this was different. It was autumn, and we were in a conference centre in the Highlands of Scotland surrounded by snowy mountain peaks. It was a little chilly at times, but I just snuggled into my favourite jumper and settled down to listen to the speaker. I don't even remember the speaker's name. I do, however, remember what he spoke on from Friday to Sunday, and I was enthralled. The speaker retold the story of Jonah, but as he did that, he was able to describe the prophet as someone who was flawed, just like us. He even disagreed with God and did his own thing. He described the sun burning down on Jonah as if God wanted to melt his heart, and I pulled my jumper tighter, sipping hot chocolate, surrounded by snow-topped firs. I have never forgotten that memory of contrasts – sun and snow, a man of faith and fear, of God's compassion and Jonah's obstinance.

I think the book of Jonah is one of my favourite books of the Old Testament, as each time I read it I come away with more things to ponder and ruminate on. It is also because it is full of high-octane drama, huge sweeping themes about forgiveness and compassion. The central character is not the fish but an experienced prophet who was also a flawed person, like the rest of us.

I really admire actors who use method acting to help them understand their characters. Method acting is a technique used by an actor who aspires to have complete emotional identification with a part. Marlon Brando and Dustin Hoffman did this. When I was writing this chapter, I think I felt a little like Jonah. I had gone out of my way to do something nice for someone. In fact, it cost me a lot to get it all sorted out, and instead of being a wonderful surprise, it had the opposite reaction. I was annoyed, upset and spent the week complaining to God about it. I felt I had done nothing wrong. It felt unjust. God spoke to me through the words of Jonah. I may have felt I had the answers but had to learn to trust Him. I was challenged about my attitude – instead of being annoyed, angry and depressed, I had to talk to God and leave it with Him. We may not go through the drama that Jonah does, but his story teaches us about how we should respond to God's plans.

**The main character**

Jonah is probably one of the best-known minor prophets, as his story is one of high drama, with near drowning, being swallowed by a large fish and the salvation of a city. It is a short book consisting of four chapters, written in a narrative style.

Jonah's story has entered the realm of folklore and nursery rhymes in today's culture. He does, however, have something important to tell us. It can appear to be an oddity – this book that is categorised as a prophetic book. Certainly, throughout the years, scholars have questioned whether Jonah should stay in the canon of Scripture.[1] Despite this, we can see that the book teaches us so much about God's love for all people. It may also seem an unusual story, but it is one that has an important message of listening to God and of God's compassion for us.

The author and speaker Colin Sinclair suggest that the book of Jonah is separated into four sections.[2] These are:

- Jonah and the storm. Jonah fled from God (chapter 1).
- Jonah and the Great fish/whale. Jonah prayed to God (chapter 2).
- Jonah and the City of Nineveh. Jonah was God's voice to the people of Nineveh (chapter 3).
- Jonah and the Lord. When Jonah learned from God (chapter 4).

Jonah is an unlikely hero who runs away instead of running to where God wanted Him to go. He seems to fail at every opportunity, but God is working in and through Jonah. Here we learn about the prophecy and the prophet. It's probably worth saying that Jonah was not fleeing from God's presence; he was fleeing from the service of God. He is not alone. I am sure we have all felt that we do not want to do what God has asked us to.

One of my greatest challenges has been to agree to speak in churches. I also love my job as a lecturer in nursing. I am happy to stand in front of more than three hundred student nurses, but ask me to speak at a church outreach or midweek meeting and I clam up and get anxious and nervous. God clearly told me a few years ago that I was not to say no when I was asked to speak at these events. When I get an email or someone phones me asking if I am available, I want to think of every excuse there is to say no. I know, though, that God has asked me to serve Him in this manner.

There have been, however, other prophets who have argued with God about His plan and what He was asking them to do. Look at Moses when God asked him to speak to Pharaoh. He had several excuses. He told God that he couldn't because of his poor speaking ability, but he was brought up in a royal household and was used to speaking to Pharaoh (Exod. 4:10). Jeremiah argued with God, as he felt he was too young to speak for Him (Jer. 1:6). Jonah didn't argue or try to talk God out of it; Jonah simply fled. In Jonah 4:11 God tells Jonah that He has concern for the city of more than a hundred and twenty thousand people who don't know God.

God called Jonah to share His message of forgiveness to the city of Nineveh. Nineveh was the capital of Assyria, rising to power in 900BC, and became the most famous city in the land in the seventh century BC because it became very prosperous as Assyria grew and developed. It seemed to have a quest of conquering Israel. By 721BC the Assyrian army had destroyed the northern kingdom of Israel. Assyria as a nation was known to be harsh, cruel and extremely brutal, even skinning their captives alive. In Nahum 2:11–13, Assyria is described as lions and lionesses, tearing and feeding on the nations. I am sure that Jonah would have liked to see its destruction rather than its deliverance. It is also worth remembering at this point that the Hebrew people proudly felt God was their very own possession – and no other's. You can understand how difficult it was for Jonah to go to Nineveh, the capital city of Judah's bitterest national enemy. It was also a Gentile city and, in effect, the 'Sin City' of that day.

Jonah was already a great prophet by the time we are properly introduced to him at the start of the book. He was a prophet of the northern kingdom of Israel in about the eighth century BC. He was considered one of the greatest prophets during the time of Jeroboam II. Jonah was the son of Amittai and, according to Jewish history and as a prophet disciple, is thought to have anointed Jehu and, therefore, enjoyed the king's benevolence.

> In the fifteenth year of Amaziah son of Joash king of Judah, Jeroboam son of Jehoash king of Israel became king in Samaria, and he reigned for forty-one years. He did evil in the eyes of the LORD and did not turn away from any of the sins of Jeroboam son of Nebat, which he had caused Israel to commit. He was the one who restored the boundaries of Israel from Lebo Hamath to the Dead Sea, in accordance with the word of the Lord, the God of Israel, spoken through his servant Jonah son of Amittai, the prophet from Gath Hepher.
>
> *(2 Kgs 14:23–25)*

## The background

The events that are recounted in the book of Jonah occurred during the reign of King Amaziah.[3] King Amaziah was a king of the southern kingdom of Judah from 797 to 796 BC although some suggest it was 803 to 775BC.[4] He succeeded his father, King Joash, who was assassinated by his own officials, so one of Amaziah's first acts was to bring justice upon the murderers of his father (2 Kgs 14:5). The Bible summarises Amaziah's reign in 2 Kings 14:3 as: 'He did what was right in the eyes of the LORD, but not as his father David had done.'

Jeroboam II (793–753BC) was the king of Israel (2 Kgs 14:25). Jonah was a prophet whose words reached the king of Judah.

The book of Jonah was probably written in between 793–758BC. There are differences of opinion concerning the historicity, and the timing of the book of Jonah and the events it describes. The questions around the dates of Jonah (and some of the other prophets) springs from uncertainty or disagreement about other key events in the Old Testament story, such as when the exodus begins, how long it lasts, the timing of the conquest, the length of period of the Judges and the reigns of each of the kings. He is, however, considered one of the oldest of the minor prophets. It is estimated that the book was written after the Babylonian Exile (sixth century BC) and certainly no later than the third century, as Jonah is listed among the minor prophets in the apocryphal book of Ecclesiasticus, composed about 190BC. Jonah lived in the Galilean city of Gath-hepher, which is approximately four miles north of Nazareth, during the reign of Jeroboam II (793–753BC), king of Israel (cf. 2 Kgs 14:25).

**The main message**

The following paragraphs are a summary of the book.

In Jonah 1, God gave Jonah a commission: a new message, but Jonah did not want to deliver it. Jonah was told to go to Nineveh. He thought he knew best and fled from God. Jonah didn't agree with God and didn't want God to forgive the people of Nineveh. We, however, don't truly understand Jonah's feelings until chapter 4. He travelled to Joppa and organised a lift on a Gentile trading vessel to Tarshish, a Phoenician colony on the south-west coast of Spain. Tarshish is probably about 2,000 miles to the west of Jonah's home and in the opposite direction to Nineveh, about 500 miles east. God only wanted Jonah to travel 500 miles to Nineveh. Two thousand miles is a long journey to flee from God rather than talk to Him.

So, he found himself on a large ship heading in a different direction. The sailors working on the boat cast off and then found themselves in the middle of an awful storm. They threw everything they could overboard to lighten the load. Jonah, however, was fast asleep in the bottom of the boat. Eventually the ship's captain found Jonah and woke him up. He shouted at Jonah for sleeping as everyone else was running around trying to save the boat and praying for the storm to stop. He told Jonah to wake up and pray to God. And all around them the storm continued to rage as if God was angry with them.

The rest of the crew knew that their prayers were not being answered and wondered if there was someone on the ship who was the reason why they were in such trouble. By this time Jonah was awake; he was cornered by frightened men asking him lots of questions, as they wanted to know why Jonah had brought all this trouble upon them. So, Jonah told them the whole story: how he came from the land of Israel, and that he tried to hide from the presence of God as he didn't want to go to Nineveh. They even asked Jonah, 'What should we do to you to make the sea calm down for us?' (v. 11).

He told the sailors to take him up to the deck and throw him into the sea. He believed that if they did that, the storm would stop and the sea would be back to normal. He knew it was his fault. Finally, as the sailors could do nothing else to save the boat and crew, they threw Jonah into the sea. As soon as Jonah was thrown into the sea, the storm instantly stopped.

You would think that Jonah would have asked God to help him. You would think he would have realised that he really needed God's help; after all, the sailors on the boat did, and they hadn't even known about God. God, not willing to give up on Jonah, sent a large, gigantic, enormous, huge beast of a fish to rescue him.

There are stories through history of sailors being swallowed by sea monsters and surviving. One example is in 1891, when a seaman called James Barley was swallowed by a large sperm whale near the Falkland Islands.[5] After three days, he was found unconscious but alive. The reporter and author investigated this story and questioned the validity of it, but there are other stories.[6] Whether you call it a big fish, whale, or sea monster, he was stuck there for three days.[7]

Then God made the fish release Jonah and told him to travel to Nineveh and warn the people of the trouble they were in so they could ask for God's help. This was God's second commission to Jonah, and Jonah did as he was asked. The journey to Nineveh would have taken more than a month. I am sure this would have given Jonah plenty of time to reflect on what had happened. So, Jonah entered the city, which was so big that it took three days to walk through, and warned the people to repent. The people believed Jonah's God. They held a great fast, wearing sackcloth and ashes. The whole city turned to God and asked forgiveness, and God heard them. Even the king heard Jonah's warning from God and covered himself in sackcloth and sat in the dust.

Despite knowing about God, being rescued from an awful storm and even the inside of a whale, Jonah was still unhappy. He still though he knew best. He thought it was all wrong. He asked God to take his life. God's reply in Jonah 4:4 is: 'Is it right for you to be angry?'

Jonah left Nineveh and stopped east of it, where he made himself a shelter and waited to see what would happen to the city. God made a leafy plant to grow over Jonah's shelter to give him some shade from the sun. Jonah waited to see what would happen next. He wanted to see the city burn.

I think God saved the city and waited to see if Jonah would understand how badly behaved he was. Jonah cared more for his plant than the hundreds of people who could have died.

God sent a worm to eat away at the plant's root, so it withered and died. Again, he did not turn to God, and losing his plant made him low and depressed. He stayed where he was and, fully exposed to the full force of the sun, felt so sad that he pleaded for God to kill him.

The book teaches us that God shows mercy to those who oppose Him. It also teaches us that He will listen to us if we feel things are not going as we want them to. There are, however, consequences if we try to do things our way. Jonah reminds us that the Lord God brought him back from a pit. Jonah nearly drowned and sank into depression, but at each turn God was listening to him.

In Judaism, the story of Jonah represents the teaching of '*teshuva*', which are teachings about forgiveness or the ability to repent and be forgiven by God. The Jewish theologian Chaim Lewis in 1972, however, said of the book of Jonah: 'It has the spaciousness of roomy oceans and big-bellied sea monsters, the brooding mystery of man and vessel caught in the coils of wind and storm, and characters oddly opposed, the one a human frailty hiding and the other a discovering Eye searching, both engaged in some fateful debate which ends as it began, with Jonah a sulking creature of defeat.'[8] He suggests that Jonah is a picture of humanity fighting the predicament of evil and forgiveness. It is a pessimistic picture and one that paints Jonah as a failing prophet. Jonah may appear frail and a failure to Chaim Lewis, but I have grown to like him.

There is something honest and real about him. Jonah is even questioning God's compassion, just like I questioned God about what happened to me. The main question of the book is, 'Are God's compassionate actions just?'[9]

Jewish theologians would suggest that Jonah was a real character, because he is mentioned in the book of Kings, and that Nineveh was a historical place. They suggest that the book of

Jonah is a '*Midrash*', which implies it is a story or some form of rabbinic instruction or a biblical version of *Aesop's Fables*.[10] In fact, Terence Fretheim, in his academic paper about the book of Jonah, suggests: 'Among the suggestions that have been made are parable, allegory, midrash, parody, satire, didactic story, ironic tale. In any case, the book is imaginative literature'.[11] R. Scott, however, suggests that the story of Jonah being swallowed by a big fish is only one of many wonders in the book.[12] Obviously, God's forgiveness is truly wondrous.

Despite what you think of him, Jonah is one of only four prophets mentioned by Jesus.

Jonah gets a mention from Jesus in Matthew 12:40. Jesus implies that the story of Jonah is accurate and calls himself 'greater than Jonah' (v. 41). He is referring to the fact that Jonah survived three nights in the depths of a whale. Jesus promises the Pharisees that they will see 'the sign of . . . Jonah' (v. 39), which is his resurrection after three days. The story of Jonah is also mentioned in Islam and the biblical narrative of Jonah is repeated, although altered slightly, in the Quran.

## About prayer

So, what does this book teach us about prayer? I think the first thing to say is that it is better to talk to God than not. In the belly of the boat Jonah didn't pray – it wasn't until he was in the belly of the whale that he turned to God. It is interesting to note that the first prayer was uttered by the sailors who did not know God, rather than Jonah. Jonah has had plenty of opportunity to pray but simply chooses not to. We are told that the sailors were praying to their gods during the storm, in Jonah 1:5. Eventually the sailors even cried out to Jonah's God, as they realised He had power over the sea and storm. The Gentile sailors prayed to the God of the Hebrews and we don't hear about Jonah praying until chapter 2 verse 2. At Jonah 2:7 he says:

> When my life was ebbing away,
> I remembered you, LORD,
> and my prayer rose to you,
> to your holy temple.

Jonah had plenty of time to reflect from the inside of the great fish. He finally prays to God. His prayer is very similar to the words of the Psalms.

It is sad that Jonah waited until then to pray, but isn't that what we do? Often, we wait until we can do nothing else; the situation is so dire that there is no way out but to pray to God. Despite this, God is still there for Jonah and ready to listen. God does not move away from us; we move away from Him. Jonah looks to God for help and is encouraged. No matter the mess we find ourselves in, whether it is because we have not done what we know God wants us to do or it is because of the place we find ourselves in, God is with us.

Certainly, the book of Jonah highlights God's patience and compassion. God teaches us that He is willing to give those who disobey Him a second chance.[13] Jesus reminds us of that in the New Testament with the parable of the lost sheep and the woman and the lost coin – see Luke 15. There is also an open channel between heaven and earth, and nothing can stop us praying, even when we get things wrong. It must have been tough for Jonah – how do you pray to God when you feel He is mute to your pleadings? Jonah was eventually honest with God. It was hard for him and I think it's also difficult in our church culture. In church, our hymns and songs are almost exclusively focused on praise and encouragement. They often include words of victory and positivity. Where do we go if we disagree, are unsure of God's plan, or generally don't understand why? In his prayer, Jonah asks for nothing; he simply cries out in acknowledgment to God. Sometimes all we can do is say His name, thank God and praise Him, without asking for anything.

I think it is also important to remember that God has no problem removing you from your comfort zone. Jonah had been God's spokesperson to his king, moving with the elite of his day. Now God wanted him to speak to a city that were his enemies, a city that was 500 miles away. In those days you could travel to Nineveh by camel or pony, but you would have to travel seventy-five miles a day. Jonah was sent to a place, miles from home and his own people. With such a challenging mission, you'd think Jonah would turn to God and ask for help. Jonah's response was the opposite. He didn't talk to God; he ran away from God. It's a powerful lesson – that even if we are unsure about God's plans for us or we are annoyed with God, we need to talk to him.

So, after all that wasted time and energy, Jonah rose and went to Nineveh as commanded. His message for the inhabitants of Nineveh was a simple one, and we are told that he said, 'Forty more days and Nineveh will be overthrown' (Jonah 3:4). Jonah had totally lost sight of what was happening here, placing his personal wishes before God's mercy. This time he prays to God in anger, revealing how he really felt:

> He prayed to the LORD, 'Isn't this what I said, LORD, when I was still at home? That is what I tried to forestall by fleeing to Tarshish. I knew that you are a gracious and compassionate God, slow to anger and abounding in love, a God who relents from sending calamity. Now, LORD, take away my life, for it is better for me to die than to live.'

*Jonah 4:2,3*

Last time, Jonah praised God. It was fine for God to save Jonah, but not for God to give the people of Nineveh another chance. But why should the people of Nineveh be treated any differently from Jonah? Jonah had to share God's word with people he didn't like. What do we do about praying for people we don't like? Matthew 5:44 says, 'But I [Jesus] tell you, love your enemies and pray for those who persecute you . . .'

Loving our enemies, praying for our enemies, equals obedience to God. The author Edward Welch, in his book *When People Are Big and God Is Small*, suggests that: 'Love for enemies is the pinnacle of obedience to God. As the Sermon on the Mount indicates, it is easy to love people who love you. But it demands a powerful work of God's Spirit to love those who are committed to harming you.'[14]

Jonah teaches us so much about God's mercy and compassion for us. He is a forgiving God who gives us a second chance, but it is also a book about prayer. It reminds us that prayer is 'an act of supplication or intercession' towards God.[15] It teaches us to be honest in prayer, to pray even though we don't know what to say or if we disagree with God. It teaches us the importance of prayer, that open communication with God is key to living life as God intends us to. It also teaches us that there are different types of prayers. Ultimately it is the pouring out of the deepest emotions of our being; and for us as Christians, it begins with knowing that, in Christ, we can come before God in prayer.[16] Prayer is so important in this little book that prayer is mentioned in every chapter.

- In chapter 1, the sailors prayed to an unknown God and He heard them (1:5).
- In chapter 2, Jonah prayed in faith (2:1–7).
- In chapter 3, the Ninevites prayed for forgiveness (3:8).

God answered every one of the prayers except Jonah's prayer recorded in chapter 4. He does, however, reply to Jonah, asking him a question. God listens to all our prayers, even if we don't know Him. He also listens to the silliest of prayers like Jonah's prayer, still angry at God. The book ends in Jonah 4:10,11 when God says:

> You have been concerned about this plant, though you did not tend it or make it grow. It sprang up overnight and died overnight. And should I not have concern for the great city of Nineveh, in which there are more than a hundred and twenty thousand people who cannot tell their right hand from their left – and also many animals?

God has the final say. He has replied to Jonah's prayer. Again, we are reminded of God's mercy for people that do not know Him.

**Let's pray**

Dear Lord,
Thank You that we can come before You.
We know that You listen to what we have to say.
Forgive us when we decide to do things our way.
Forgive us when we think we have all the answers.
Help us to trust You – to remember Your ways are higher than ours.
In Jesus' name.
Amen.

# A Cry for Justice

*Anna Arnold*

The sun was pounding down on my skin and the air was heavy with an uncomfortable heat that made you want to jump head-first into a pool of freezing cold water. There was no water nearby, only a tree which I was using as a makeshift head rest as I watched kids in the field below sprint towards a beaten-up football.

It was August 2010 and my family and I were one week into our mission trip to Uganda. It felt like I had already learned more in one week than I had in my entire twelve years of existence. And as a 12-year-old, I thought I already knew quite a lot. It was fair to say my world had drastically changed and I was going home completely different. I had encountered the harsh realities of poverty for the first time, and I wasn't sure how to react or how to help the people in front of me. I knew that I could not ignore how my heart felt towards the people I had met. I knew that I wanted to show love, to care and to help people in what-ever way I could. As I sat by the tree, I listened to laughter and shouting as one of the teams missed yet another goal.

A gentle breeze had picked up around me, and I began to straighten up in the heavy heat. Almost immediately, a flurry of images flooded my mind like a scene out of a stop motion video. I saw a picture of a child being whipped and a figure moving towards the child to hold them, to protect them. It was like a gentle daydream, and as I tried to figure out what I was seeing, I sensed God saying, 'Anna, protect my children.'

I was interrupted. I didn't know what any of this meant. I laughed at the thought of under 5ft me (at the time) helping or protecting anyone. I had already ruled myself out, and I nearly missed what God was saying.

'I am not a protector, I'm a 12-year-old. I can barely look after myself!' I wanted to say.

It wasn't until we returned home that I realised the power of this moment. On a long, hot summer day in Uganda, God had begun to reveal His heart for justice to me. I was introduced to the God of justice who is wildly passionate about the oppressed, the marginalised and the rejected.[1]

## The main character

Somewhat unexpectedly, mixed within the story of Amos, we discover that he was a shepherd. To give some perspective, during Amos's lifetime, a shepherd was not somebody society treated well. In fact, the role of a shepherd was isolating by nature and included being on the outskirts of social hubs and living in the wilderness to watch after a flock. Amos would have been doing the job that a) no one wanted to do and b) the people around him looked down upon. The mention of his career gives the impression that Amos was somebody who had most probably already been ruled out by many around him. He was not a well-known great preacher, and he was definitely not somebody with an impressive résumé of public speaking experience. Even more surprisingly, he was from Tekoa, a wild and stony district in the south of Jerusalem. Amos was a foreigner in Israel. He was from the south but speaking into the north, fuelling another reason for those listening to disregard his voice. So, at the beginning of the book we are introduced to Amos the 'unlikely prophet'.

## The background

Amos was delivered around 760–750BC when Amos's words were spoken into a thriving and bustling Israel. Under the reign of Jeroboam II, the nation was experiencing the height of its power so far. Israel had expanded their territory to create trade routes to the ruling empires of Assyria and Egypt, and with access to these routes came tax revenue and what appeared to be great prosperity. Yet, below the surface, the people of Israel were suffering. God's chosen people were quenched. Idols, false religion and the overwhelming weight of oppression were crippling society and creating spiritual drought. Amos's message was pivotal – it was time the people of Israel were to:

> Seek good, not evil, that you may live.
> Then the LORD God almighty will be with you, just as you say he is.
> Hate evil, love good; maintain justice in the courts.
>
> *Amos 5:14,15a*

The structure of Amos's message can be summarised as a passionate plea to God's people to a) look at what is around them, b) look at what is within them, and c) look at what is to come. Amos called out what God saw as unjust, he reminded the people of Israel of their wrongdoing, and he warned them of the consequences of ignoring God's justice. When you read this narrative, it almost feels as though you are interrupting a raw and painful conversation between a Father and his children who, simply put, have strayed and walked completely away from Him.

## The main message

As we explore the book of Amos, I pray that you will draw closer to God and be challenged and transformed by His compassion and love. God who gently encouraged me in 2010 is the same God who has spoken to generations through the minor prophets and He is the same God who wants to speak to you today.

When my mum first asked me to write a chapter about Amos in a book about prayer, I was confused. I wasn't sure what to write. Amos wouldn't have been my go-to place to discover more about prayer. Although the word 'justice' only appears seven times in this book, Amos deals with lots of social injustices that exist today.[2] Because of this, the book of Amos has become a focal point used in churches to discuss justice. Grand, poetic verses like 'let justice roll on like a river, righteousness like a never-failing stream!' (Amos 5:24) jump off the page, revealing God's heart for justice.

The book of Amos is filled with challenge, anguish, lament and hope. It is a rollercoaster of exchanges, a warning to a nation and a cry for justice. And this book teaches us valuable lessons about prayer. As we read, we discover that God:

1. Redefines expectations
2. Relentlessly pursues justice
3. Restores situations

Ultimately, teaching us three lessons about God that in turn should impact our prayer life.

So, let's begin at the very start of the book.

### *God redefines expectations*

The words of Amos, one of the shepherds of Tekoa – the vision
j he saw concerning Israel two years before the earthquake, when Uzziah was king of Judah and Jeroboam son of Jehoash was king of Israel.

Amos chapter 1 verse 1 sets the scene. We discover that Amos is prophesying to Israel under the reign of Jeroboam two years before the 'earthquake', providing details that help us pinpoint a timeline for his ministry.[3] This timeline paints a picture of the culture and context Amos was speaking into. There is a simple lesson in this text that should encourage us. God calls the unexpected and He redefines expectations. Amos is a character, like so many others in the Bible, who was rejected and mocked by society. Those listening to him probably had very low expectations of him. Yet, God chose a rejected and forgotten man to be His voice into Israel at a pivotal point in history. Whilst this may not be new information to you, it is important to press into the lesson that God redefines expectations.

I have met so many people in my life who reflect this lesson in Amos to me. The truth is Amos was available. He gave up where he was and what he was doing to follow God. It is easy to believe the lie that we cannot be used by God. But the truth is we can, more often than not; we just need to make ourselves available. What would happen if we held onto the truth that God redefines expectations, and what would happen if we gave

Him the opportunity to show this? Where the world sees inadequacy, or the impossible, our Father welcomes expectancy.

In 2017 I visited the Middle East. Whilst I was volunteering at a children's holiday club, I met a 6-year-old girl called Grace.[4] As the morning session came to a close, I sat with Grace and the other children as a team leader began to chat with the kids in Arabic. One of the translators explained that these children were about to pray. These kids were amazing; they had come from families who fled Syria during the civil war, and they had experienced trauma beyond imagination. As the children began praying, Grace smiled and said a few sentences and the circle fell silent. The translator turned to me and explained what Grace had prayed. She asked God that the men with guns, who had shot her dad in front of her, would stop shooting and that we would forgive them. She was only young and she was full of courage.

Amos, the unexpected prophet, Grace a 6-year-old girl and Anna, a 12-year-old trying to make sense of the world around her. These stories are threaded together by a God who redefines expectations and who uses the people who are often on the side or who don't 'fit the bill'.

**About prayer**

What would it look like if:

1. We prayed believing that God redefines expectations and uses our voice?
2. We prayed and allowed God the space to interrupt out lives?

Our prayers change when we know the truth of who we are praying to. We don't pray expecting God to ignore us. We pray confidently because God chooses to use us. He shows his glory by redefining expectations. We can come to God asking him to do 'immeasurably more than all we ask or imagine, according to his power that is at work within us' (Eph. 3:20).

I shared Grace's story for two reasons. First, she used her voice. Despite her age and a language barrier, Grace spoke up and prayed what was on her heart. Second, Grace's prayer was simple. She didn't prophesy into a nation using complex imagery, like Amos, but she spoke from where she was at. In doing so her impact was greater than she could have realised. God continues to surprise us by using the unexpected. Be encouraged that you have purpose and God wants to reveal that to you. Do your own expectations need to be redefined? Do you need to give God space this week to interrupt you? As you pray, allow yourself to learn the truth that God redefines expectations.

### God relentlessly pursues justice

In chapters 1 and 2, Amos begins his prophetic words by addressing the regions surrounding Israel. Amos deals with Damascus,[5] Gaza,[6] Tyre[7], Edom,[8] Ammon,[9] Moab[10] and Judah.[11] He calls out underlying injustices, oppression and exploitation within these nations. He deals with social issues such as slavery, murder, deceit and false religion. We read 'for three sins of [insert region], even for four, I will not relent' before Amos addresses each nation to the volume of unjust actions happening in these regions. By chapter 2, Amos has built up to the inevitable judgment of Israel. He calls out

God's frustration with the people of Israel as: 'They trample on the heads of the poor as on the dust of the ground and deny justice to the oppressed' (v. 7). We are introduced to the brokenness within these nations and the concern of a just and fair God.

Israel, the people who had once followed justice systems in the wilderness, had become wild.[12] They were a nation who accepted bribery within the courts and lost sight of good and evil.[13] '"They do not know how to do right," declares the LORD, "who store up in their fortresses what they have plundered and looted"' (Amos 3:10). The chapters are loaded with anguish and frustration as God watches his people consistently disregard those around them. It is clear why this book has become a natural 'focal point for discussions about social injustice'.[14]

Challengingly, Amos is addressing issues that exist today. For example, he speaks about communities in slavery in the regions of Gaza and Tyre.[15] Amos provides us with insight as to how God feels about oppression, and the reality is these same oppressions exist today. Israel thousands of years ago is not too dissimilar to the world we live in now. The social injustices that frustrated God then, exist now.

Last year I had the opportunity to work with an organisation called International Justice Mission (IJM). IJM work in communities across the globe to end modern day slavery in our lifetime.[16] They work tirelessly to rescue victims, restore survivors, restrain criminals and repair justice systems. IJM operates across the world bringing men, women and children out of forced labour, trafficking and sexual exploitation. There is a demanding need for the work of IJM because the reality is the world is a dark and broken place. Today, more than 40 million people are trapped in modern-day slavery.[17] This figure is staggering and it is hard to digest that 40 million men, women and children are in situations where they are exploited and stripped of their true dignity. How do we respond when we hear the scale of injustice like this?

In the book, *Generous Justice* by Timothy Keller, Gary Haugen – the founder of IJM – describes a child's fascination with a new toy and how a child loses interest when this toy is removed from their eyesight.[18] He compares this to our ability to engage with modern issues of social injustice. Often our response to social injustice is immediate emotion. We are moved by a story we have read and we feel the need within our hearts to do something, to respond, to help in whatever way we can. But we turn away from what we have read, we become distracted and the emotions that had risen up in us gently simmer away. When we are confronted with injustice, how do we respond? I have experienced this time and time again. I remember returning home from the mission trips with raw waves of emotion in response to the injustice I have seen. But, quickly, the waves of these emotions settle down and I begin complaining about bad wi-fi despite meeting people who have nothing a week before. We are quick to detach ourselves from injustice as we aren't confronted with it day to day. How do we maintain a healthy and consistent response to justice?

Timothy Keller suggests that there is a more mature way for Christians to engage with injustice. He discusses that we should:

1. Consider what justice is, viewing it from the perspective of those affected by injustice.
2. Consider what justice looks like, viewing it from God's perspective. We do this by considering it through the lens of Scripture.

Amos points us to God's heart for equality, fairness and justice. We don't need to try to convince God to move, He already wants to. In fact, prayer looks less like us changing God's heart and more like Him changing ours. When we pray effectively, we draw close to God in conversation and, ultimately, come away desiring the things He desires not having just finished a pitch to some entitled investor. Instead, we pray to a God who already cares. When we pray for justice, we are praying for desires of God's heart, and we begin to look more like Him.

The likelihood is that, if you are somebody who is reading this book, you can relate to Haugen's example of the toy in front of the child. To engage with issues of social justice, we need to engage with God. To pray for social justice, we need to look to God. It is encouraging that as you and I pray for our world, our perspective changes.

In Psalm 37:4 the psalmist expresses: 'Take delight in the LORD, and he will give you the desires of your heart.' As we spend time with God, our desires change. We long for God and His desires. Amos teaches us that God relentlessly pursues justice, and this becomes our desire.

This week allow yourself the space to reflect, to stop and to spend time with God. If you feel detached and lethargic towards news headlines of oppression, spend time with God and your heart will align to His heart for justice.

### God restores situations

One of the major narrative themes we discover in the book of Amos is his continual call to the Israelites to return to God. At face value, this moment for the Israelite community feels like a far cry from the courageous and chosen people who once marched between the towering walls of the Red Sea towards their promised inheritance during the period of the exodus. Yet, as we continue to navigate our way through the narrative of the Old Testament, we find this 'turning away from God' to be an all-too-familiar trait in the story. It never seems to be too long before the same people who praised God for the miraculous were cursing the fact they were ever made.

Chapter 5 brings us into a moment of Amos's petition for Israel's repentance. He shocks those around him by beginning to sing a lamentful song for the people, as though they had been destroyed. In the moment, Amos doesn't hold back from reminding the Israelites of the truth:

> This is what the LORD says to Israel:
> 'Seek me and live;
> do not seek Bethel,
> do not go to Gilgal,
> do not journey to Beersheba.'

*Amos 5:4,5*

'Seek me and live'. This is explicit, raw and weighty. It packs a strong punch! The heart of Amos's lament is so simple yet incredibly profound – true life is found only in the whole-hearted pursuit of God! This is a revelation of the heart of God in that His deep desire is to be sought by His people above anything and everything else. The sad reality was that the Israelites had forgotten who they were and why they existed. They had lost sight of God as the great desire and treasure of their hearts. Their posture had become insular as they began to worship their wealth and multiple false gods. This is why the lament reads 'do not seek Bethel, do not seek Gilgal, do not journey to

Beersheba', as many scholars recognise these cities as symbols of idolatry for the Israelite people.

The poignancy of this moment for the Israelite community is especially astounding when you consider the point in history in which this moment occurred.

This was a community of people who had experienced the blessing, power and favour of God generationally for hundreds of years. They would have had more stories than most of us could ever dream of having regarding God's faithfulness and love. Yet, somehow, it was not enough for them. Once again, their hearts had become cold and indifferent towards the presence of God.

Throughout the narrative of Amos, we begin to get a fuller picture of God's frustration with their passivity towards Him. In chapter 7, we read a 'warning vision' given to Amos by God regarding the spiritual state of the Israelite community:

> The high places of Isaac will be destroyed
> and the sanctuaries of Israel will be ruined;
> with my sword I will rise against the house of Jeroboam
>
> *Amos 7:9*

As if this isn't enough, Amos receives another vision from God in chapter 8! This time, it's a picture of a basket of fruit symbolising the internal rottenness of the Israelites through selfishness and oppression. In this moment, Israel were materially wealthy yet in spiritual poverty. Their wallets were full; however, their hearts had become empty.

All of this really frustrates me. I mean, how could they turn from God after all He had done for them? This was a community with an incredibly rich spiritual heritage! As we've already thought about, they would've had a lifetime's worth of stories testifying to the loving kindness of God towards them. It seems so ridiculous that they would have the capacity to allow themselves to become distant to God. Yet, even as I write these words, the Israelite complex sounds awfully familiar to me. Actually, it reads much like the narrative of my own life at times. How many times have I chosen to step away from God and do what I think is right, what I want to do? How many times have I lost sight of the fact that God is good? When have I chosen money, love, or feeling good above what is right and just?

In so many ways, these people were no different to you and me. We've all fallen short more times than we would like to admit. We've all had moments where we've willingly chosen to reject God and go our own way. The beautiful reality underpinning this story lies in the wider narrative of the Scriptures – God is the ultimate restorer of bad situations. He can take the most broken, damaged and imperfect goods and radically transform them into their original, intended design. Nothing is 'too far gone' for His love. In this story, we are reminded of God's ultimate heart for His creation: 'He who was seated on the throne said, "I am making everything new!"' (Rev. 21:5).

In Amos 9:14,15, God reveals His heart to restore His people:

'I will bring my people Israel back from exile.

They will rebuild the ruined cities and live in them.

They will plant vineyards and drink their wine; they will make gardens and eat their fruit.

I will plant Israel in their own land, never again to be uprooted from the land I have given them,' says the LORD your God.

Mull these words over. It's the restorative heart of our loving Father on full display! In His kingdom, mercy always 'triumphs over judgment' (Jas 2:13). God always has the final word.

This is the good news at the heart of the book of Amos – our disobedience cannot invalidate the heart of the Father towards us. Our indifference is no match for his wild passion for us. He carries within Himself an unrelenting desire to restore us to the originality of His design for us. In Jesus Christ, the redemptive and restorative heart of God has fully restored us as perfect and beautiful in His sight – we have become a new humanity. We are reminded of Paul's words to the church in Colossae:

> Once you were alienated from God and were enemies in your minds because of your evil behaviour. But now he has reconciled you by Christ's physical body through death to present you holy in his sight, without blemish and free from accusation . . .
>
> *Col. 1:21,22*

When we pray, we pray to the God who restores the world. We don't pray to a detached or frustrated Father. God draws us close – there is nothing between us. We can pray openly and honestly. We are accepted as we are because we can have a relationship with him. We can bring situations that don't make sense and our questions; God longs to restore us. He is the restorer, and today there may be things in your life that need restoring.

The book of Amos teaches us that God:

1. Redefines expectations.[19]
2. Relentlessly pursues justice. [20]
3. Restores situations.[21]

We pray differently because we are transformed by God.

**Let's pray**

Thank You, Father,
that you have a perfect plan for the world around us.
We are sorry that we are fractured and broken, that we don't
care for the people in the world around us as we should.
Help us to speak out and do what you would have us do.
Help us to be an advocate for the weak, the vulnerable, for
those who do not feel they have a voice.
Help us to live justly and love mercy as You do.
In Jesus' name.
Amen.

# 3
## Hosea

# A Cry to Be Faithful

*Cathy Le Feuvre*

We know, when we immerse ourselves in the Old Testament, that we're entering a number of intriguing worlds. We are learning about the history of God's chosen people, Israel. Their heritage, culture and practices handed down the centuries even to current generations.

The Old Testament also contains the most fascinating and challenging personal stories of individuals. These include those who followed, or tried to follow, God, Jehovah, or Yahweh as the Jews originally knew the Almighty Being, as well as those who did not and indeed those who fought against God, His Law and people. Many of the men, women and children whose names and narratives have been handed down to us through the pages of the Old Testament struggled with the same issues that you and I may face today. The individuals we read about in the thirty-nine books of the Old Testament reflect even modern differing opinions of God and faith, belief and non-belief, say!

But the books of the Old Testament – and the stories of the prophets of old in particular – also include not just handed down stories of history and people but aspects of culture and philosophy that may sometimes be lost on today's readers.

There are great chunks of poetry, exquisite prose, allegory, symbolism and prophecy which can sometimes be hard to decipher. Yet when we try to unravel the mysteries of some of the more challenging aspects of these ancient writings, we begin to understand more about not just the people who they relate to but the very nature of a God who cares about His creation.

## The main character

The book which carries HIS story is thought to be in part a narrative of the writer's own life and relationships, and a metaphor, a prophecy and a challenge for the people of his time and ours. We know extraordinarily little about the man Hosea. At the very start of his 'book' we learn that he was the son of someone called Beeri, but apart from that we have little personal history before he starts writing. We do know, however, from that first verse, that he lived in the northern kingdom of Israel towards the end of the long reign of King Jeroboam II and the very turbulent period which followed.

And we also know that his name – Hosea – in Hebrew can be translated as 'salvation', and that also tells us something exciting about his prophecies and the story he has to tell.

## The background

It's thought our prophet Hosea lived and wrote throughout that turbulent period. Looking at that first verse of the book of Hosea and the list of kings during his time, it's reckoned he was living and writing over a period of forty years and more. This is some background to the time period.

The reign of Jeroboam II is thought to have lasted more than forty years in the eighth century BC. The actual dates are disputed by scholars, with some saying he reigned from about 789 to 748BC. But whatever the specifics, what we do understand is during Jeroboam II's long reign, the northern kingdom of which he was ruler prospered, partially because it engaged in conflict and conquered other kingdoms around it. However, with success came spiritual decline, the worship of idols, a move away from Jehovah and his law. People began to depend more on their own understanding and initiatives rather than relying on God for wisdom, guidance and truth.

Some say Jeroboam II was, towards the end of his rule, the worst of the kings of Israel because, after a great start when he ran a stable government, as the years progressed, he lost interest not just in God but also in his people's faith life. He allowed those for whom he had responsibility to move so far away from their God that they not only turned to idolatry, but their behaviour – unlawful sex, murder, theft, cheating – put them on course for separation from God and spiritual, economic and political disaster.

After King Jeroboam II's death, his son Zechariah only ruled for about six months before he was assassinated by a chancer called Shallum. Just a month later Shallum was killed by Menahem, one of his military commanders, who was assisted by the king of the nation of Assyria, Tilglath-pileser III. When Menahem died a few years later, his son Pekahiah reigned for just two years before he too was murdered by one of his generals, Pekah, who then claimed the throne for himself.

They were uncertain times for anyone in power in that part of the world and Pekah knew he needed help if he was to secure his authority. He had, apparently, been opposed to that alliance with Assyria in previous years and chose to join forces with

Assyria's enemy, Egypt. In fact, he allied himself with Rezin of Damascus in an expedition against Ahaz, king of Judah, the southern kingdom. Ahaz turned to Assyria and Tilglath-Pileser III (who had been waiting on the sidelines for his opportunity), and invaded Galilee and Gilead, regions of the northern kingdom. Its inhabitants were taken into captivity.

Pekah didn't last much longer on the seat of power. Within a few years he, too, fell victim to a conspiracy headed by Hoshea (not to be confused with Hosea) who the Assyrians recognised as king of the northern kingdom. After the death of Tilglath-Pileser III, Hoshea decided to split with the Assyrians and went in with the mortal enemies, Egypt, which led to another invasion – this time of the region of Samaria – by the Assyrians. And the kingdom of Israel was effectively over.

The book and prophecies of Hosea are believed to be among the world's first literary writings. As with other prophets who came before him, Hosea probably first delivered his prophecies orally. But then they were written down – possibly even by Hosea, perhaps towards the end of his life. Hosea is thought to be one of the first examples of oral prophecies being deliberately collected and collated for future generations.

As we explore a relationship with the Almighty, it's worth considering this heritage. Down the millennia since those times, hundreds of years even before He sent his Son to the world, God was weaving his message into history, leaving us glimpses of His love and compassion and care for the world which He had created, which He loved, but which was falling away from Him.

So, Hosea stood on the side lines of history, watching and commenting and foretelling what was to come. And although from ancient times Hosea has been a bit of a prophet of doom and destruction, underlying it all is a promise of salvation and restoration for the people of Israel. This is so encouraging for us as we consider the book. While all around him was chaos, part of what Hosea was saying was that, although the people of Israel had forgotten God as their first love and this political turmoil, invasion and disaster was the result, there was still hope. Love would ultimately win over sin.

Hosea's message wasn't just rhetorical. It is also thought to be based in fact. Just like today's Christian teachers who often take examples from everyday life to deliver a message, Hosea drew from his own experiences, and his prophecy is effectively a symbolic representation of God and his people, Israel.

**The main message**

At the heart of Hosea's story is his own love life.

We first hear from Hosea as he starts life as a married man. His wife was a woman called Gomer, and from the beginning of their relationship he knew that she was flawed. In fact, she was a bit of a good-time girl. She may even have already been a 'prostitute' when she got together with Hosea, although some modern commentators have inferred that perhaps the description of Gomer as a 'wife of whoredom' is anticipating what she would become.[1] Whatever the case, she wasn't the ideal partner for a man of God, and you'd think Hosea would steer clear away from such a woman. But no. In fact, it appears that he deliberately found and married her, because God told him to do so. Hosea 1:3–5 says:

> So he married Gomer daughter of Diblaim, and she conceived and bore him a son.
>     Then the LORD said to Hosea, 'Call him Jezreel, because I will soon punish the house of Jehu for the massacre at Jezreel, and I will put an end to the kingdom of Israel. In that day I will break Israel's bow in the Valley of Jezreel.'

From the very start of his marriage, Hosea found himself mirroring the relationship of God to the people of Israel. Jehovah knew His people were inconsistent and had even 'prostituted' their relationship with Him through their worship of idols, errant behaviour and selfishness, but still he loved them.

It wasn't enough that God wanted Hosea to experience that same relationship through his marriage with Gomer; the children who came afterwards also seemed to have a purpose in the prophecy to come.'[2]

It seems inconceivable to a modern reader and believer that a holy man like Hosea would enter such a relationship, knowing that it was likely to go horribly wrong. But that, indeed, is what happened.

Some scholars say that perhaps, at the time of their marriage, Gomer had promised to be a loyal wife and that the early years of their marriage, certainly until the birth of their first child, were happy.[3] But then, it seems, she may well have been up to her old ways. The fact that he gave the two younger children their unusual names 'not loved' and 'not my people' could indicate that he feared they weren't, actually, his offspring!

It might be interesting at this point to consider Gomer's perspective in all this. In his book *Hosea*, which explores the prophet and his times from a feminist, psychoanalytical and poetic perspective, Francis Landy[4] even suggests that it must have been hard to be married to Hosea, a man who is working out his divine commandments from God through his own marriage. Imagine trying to keep the family together while your husband gives such appalling names to your children and you are being held up as the example of Israel's infidelity towards God. Keeping it together must have been tricky to say the least – that's if Gomer was aware of what Hosea was doing.

Near the start of chapter 2, we start to move from direct personal narrative to Hosea's prophecy of the relationship between Jehovah and Israel as if the nation were God's spouse. But there's no doubting that it could also be a reflection of Hosea's own relationship with Gomer and the children.

Rebuke your mother, rebuke her, for she is not my wife, and I am not her husband.

Let her remove the adulterous look from her face and the unfaithfulness from between her breasts.

Otherwise I will strip her naked and make her as bare as on the day she was born;

I will make her like a desert, turn her into a parched land, and slay her with thirst.

I will not show my love to her children, because they are the children of adultery.

Their mother has been unfaithful and has conceived them in disgrace.

She said, 'I will go after my lovers, who give me my food and my water, my wool and my linen, my olive oil and my drink.'

*Hos. 2:2–5*

Yes, the worst appeared to have happened. Gomer had left the marriage and gone with other men; she had 'committed adultery' – broken the seventh of the Ten Commandments laid down for the people of Israel during the time of Moses. Worse than that, it seemed she'd been sold into slavery or at least had got into some serious debt.

The book of Hosea can be split roughly into several sections and the first, chapters 1 to 3, are basically about the relationship of Hosea with Gomer and his own family, and in chapter 3 we read how the prophet is urged to forgive her and to reach out to her.

> The LORD said to me, 'Go, show your love to your wife again, though she is loved by another man and is an adulteress. Love her as the LORD loves the Israelites, though they turn to other gods and love the sacred raisin cakes.'
>
> So I bought her for fifteen shekels of silver and about a homer and a lethek of barley. Then I told her, 'You are to live with me for many days; you must not be a prostitute or be intimate with any man, and I will behave the same way toward you.'
>
> *Hos. 3:1–3*

Hosea had gone through the mill with his unfaithful wife but, with God's help, had survived the turmoil, and he entered a period of reconciliation and forgiveness.

This, we know, is not just a tale of marital infidelity. The situation in which Hosea found himself is also a metaphor for the relationship between God and His creation, his people. And once we plough through the mass of complex prose and poetry, and at times abrupt but beautifully figurative images and symbolic allegory, we can begin to understand some eternal truths.

Hosea's message can be summarised in quite simple terms – God loves His people, even though they are sinful and they have not put God first.[5]

Even though the people of Israel had apparently abandoned any religious belief and even turned to worshipping idols, God wasn't giving up on them. He still loved them and still had faith that they would return to Him. And that's still the same today!

The book of Hosea goes on for fourteen chapters, during which we hear all about the wrongs that Israel was getting into, which were taking them further and further away from Jehovah. We hear not just about their sins, but the judgment that was due them. We also hear commentary on the socio-economic and even political times although they are deeply embedded in the text.

We begin to understand the pain which Israel's actions and their turning to idols cause God, and the mercy which He is always willing to show. That is the overall conclusion in the third section of Hosea's prophecies, outlined in chapters 11 to 14.

> I will not carry out my fierce anger, nor will I devastate Ephraim again.
>> For I am God, and not a man – the Holy One among you.
>> I will not come against their cities.
>> They will follow the LORD; he will roar like a lion.
>> When he roars, his children will come trembling from the west.
>> They will come from Egypt, trembling like sparrows, from Assyria, fluttering like doves.
>> I will settle them in their homes,' declares the LORD.
>
> *Hos. 11:9–11*

It can all be rather depressing, especially if we just consume just the words. Hosea's use of language can be beautiful but it also is uncompromising. He pulls no punches, scattering his prophecies with the truth of what the people of Israel have been up to – adultery, cursing, lying, murder, misery, defiled . . . the list goes on.

But even as the family side of his story is concluding in chapter 3, and Hosea begins to launch into that wider prophetic interpretation of his personal history, he has an early glimmer of hope.

For the Israelites will live for many days without king or prince, without sacrifice or sacred stones, without ephod or household gods. Afterwards the Israelites will return and seek the LORD their God and David their king. They will come trembling to the LORD and to his blessings in the last days.

*Hos. 3: 4,5*

## About prayer

Down the centuries, Hosea has been the source of inspiration for many Christians. Charles Haddon Spurgeon wrote many sermons on the book of Hosea and of course, he and others have linked the promise of God's salvation in the book of Hosea with the salvation of Jesus Christ, His Son. Did you know that Hosea's story has even been the inspiration for a stage musical? It seems unlike given the nature of the tale, its underlying themes, language and the allegory. But it's true.

In the late 1960s popular music was undergoing dramatic changes – think rock and roll – and stage musicals were beginning to impact on culture, especially in the USA, the UK and increasingly across the globe. One of the first shows which commented on the politics and culture of the day, and the lives of young people especially, was the hugely popular *Hair*, which first saw the light of day in New York in late 1967. *Cabaret* and *Sweet Charity* had first been debuted the year before, and it wouldn't be long before musicians and lyricists were even taking on biblical themes for their rock opera creations. The best known of these have to be *Jesus Christ Superstar* (1970) and *Godspell* (1971).

It was in the mid-1960s that The Salvation Army in the UK, aware of this cultural wind of change, asked two young 'officers' – ministers of The Salvation Army – who they knew had musical and poetic talents, to write and produce some stage shows which would inspire audiences, involve church members in performances and reflect biblical principles as well as relevant cultural issues and questions.

The musician John Larsson and writer/poet/lyricist John Gowans both went on, separately, to be the General, the leader of the international Salvation Army. From 1967 to 1990, in addition to their duties as local church and mission leaders, they created ten musicals: stage shows based on the Bible, modern society, church and Salvation Army culture.

Many of the songs they wrote for the shows are so loved and popular that they have made it into the Salvation Army 'songbook', or hymn book. And some of those are from their second stage musical, based on the story of the prophet Hosea.

Although the story and prophecies of Hosea don't necessarily sit comfortably with a modern audience, Gowans and Larsson found a way to weave the tale into a show which was first performed in autumn 1969. They 'stole' a Shakespearean theatrical device of writing a 'play within a play'. In this case, they have the story of a group of young Christians who decide to put on a play and *Hosea* is the result. Set in modern times, with its themes of the unfaithfulness of people and a faithful God, it struck chords with audiences across the UK.[6]

One of the enduring songs from the musical may be simple in its wording and message but it clearly encapsulates the message that the prophet Hosea was given to share with the world all those centuries ago. It is about the fact that you cannot stop God from loving you no matter what you do, whether you disobey Him or betray Him. He never ever stops loving us.[7]

What Hosea had to say to his own time is still relevant, not just to our twenty-first century culture, but to each of us flawed individuals. No matter how far we move away from Him, God is always willing to welcome us back. In a judgmental world where forgiveness can appear to be in short supply, where harsh critics hide behind social media handles and purposefully choose to throw all kinds of accusations at those with whom they disagree, it's good to remember that, however nasty the world becomes, God has plans for it to return to the perfection He first created. And however much we turn our back on Him, God has plans for a relationship with all of us.

When interpreting Hosea's prophecies and writing, some writers have fixated on the story of the unfaithfulness of Gomer and have used it to speak theologically into issues of adultery and divorce. But as we've learned, it's much more than that. Hosea was writing at a time when the people of the northern kingdom had not only turned from God but were worshipping other gods instead.

There's a lesson in there for us all and questions to be asked. Are there 'idols' in our lives which are taking the place of God? Unlike Hosea's contemporaries, we might not be murdering or stealing or cheating or getting up to all sorts of depraved behaviour, but do we have attitudes, relationships, possessions, habits, beliefs, convictions or thoughts which are keeping us from a living relationship with Jesus Christ and His Father?

As we look at the life, times and prophecies of Hosea, we can be assured that God is always willing to forgive, to heal and to welcome us 'home', no matter how far we have moved away from Him. Even if we've deliberately turned our backs on Him, He is just waiting for us to return to His love. We, though, need to acknowledge our sins and wrongdoings and be willing to approach Him in penitence.

As Hosea writes in his final chapter:

Return, Israel, to the LORD your God. Your sins have been your downfall!

Take words with you and return to the LORD.

Say to him: 'Forgive all our sins and receive us graciously, that we may offer the fruit of our lips. Assyria cannot save us; we will not mount war-horses.

We will never again say "Our gods" to what our own hands have made, for in you the fatherless find compassion.'

'I will heal their waywardness and love them freely, for my anger has turned away from them.

I will be like the dew to Israel; he will blossom like a lily.

Like a cedar of Lebanon he will send down his roots; his young shoots will grow.

His splendour will be like an olive tree, his fragrance like a cedar of Lebanon.

People will dwell again in his shade; they will flourish like the corn, they will blossom like the vine – Israel's fame will be like the wine of Lebanon.

Ephraim, what more have I to do with idols? I will answer him and care for him.

I am like a flourishing juniper; your fruitfulness comes from me.'

Who is wise? Let them realise these things. Who is discerning? Let them understand.

The ways of the Lord are right; the righteous walk in them, but the rebellious stumble in them.

**Let's pray**

Oh Lord,

We're sorry that we allow things to come between us and Your great love.

We're sorry that we have dishonoured You with some of our choices.

Whatever 'idols' we have in our lives, help us to see through them and to cast them aside so that we might live as You would wish us to.

Help us to rely entirely on You rather than on the things of this world which can so easily let us down.

If we have disappointed You in our attitudes and relationships, please forgive us.

If we have forgotten how fortunate we are to live in a world made by You, remind us of the importance of looking after Your creation.

In a world where faithfulness can sometimes be in short supply, help us to be faithful and to live faithfully.

In a world where insincerity, superficiality, judgment and unkindness is all around, help us to be sincere, kind, encouraging and understanding as we go deeper into our relationship with You and with others.

Thank You for not giving up on us, whatever we do to disappoint You or let You down.

We pray for families ripped apart by separation, divorce, uncertainty and distance.

We pray for those struggling with their relationships and marriages.

We pray for children living in distress and without the certainty of home.

Bring peace and reconciliation, comfort and security.

And help us to be part of Your solution in our world.
O God, draw us closer to You
every moment
every day.
Amen

# 4
## Nahum

# Repentance

I did not know a lot about Nahum before I started writing about him. It is a book I often find difficult to locate when searching the Old Testament. As I read it again and again, I began to really appreciate the words, their style, and the message of the book. In fact, when you start reading, you can be put off by the words, 'The LORD is a jealous and avenging God' (Nah. 1:2). Maybe it is because we do not describe God in those words any more. We focus on His love and mercy.

I dream a lot but do not always remember the dreams I have. Usually, they are a real mix of colours, words and fragments of pictures. I have, however, had a couple of dreams that have stood out through the years. In the weeks leading up to coming to faith, there is one dream that stands out.

I was in an impressive building. It was a church, the size and shape of a cathedral, but it was full of people. Some of them were hanging off pillars, like they did in the photos of VE day in Trafalgar square. Some of them were pushing and shoving others, trying to get to the front of the crowd. I slowly stepped back thinking I had to let other people in front of me. I knew God was coming to visit the cathedral but thought I was being godly, letting others see Him first.

I remember the feeling of excitement as God got closer. The rumbling of voices got louder and louder and then there was silence. Everything stopped. People moved to the side and a runway opened in front of me. I turned to see what was happening and heard God speak to me. He had stopped in front of me and called my name. 'Debbie, stop putting people in the way of getting to know Me more.' Those are the words I heard. I woke up remembering everything about that dream apart from how He sounded. In that moment I understood what He meant and that He is a jealous God. He wanted me to know Him, and he wanted me to do everything I could to push the crowds out of the way and run towards Him. He is a jealous God and has every right to be.

'Jealous God' is one of the names of God and can be difficult to understand. The Hebrew word for 'jealous' also means 'zealous'. God is a zealous God wanting the best for His children. When God sees us wandering away from Him, He calls us back into a relationship with Him. Nahum tells us the story of God who loves His people and wants a right relationship with us.

**The main character**

We do not know a lot about Nahum. In fact, we know more about his message of repentance and who he was speaking to than about him. Nahum also had a message for the people of Judah as God had pronounced judgment and the Assyrians would soon be getting just what they deserved. In some ways, the message to the Hebrew people is one of comfort. In fact, Nahum's name means 'comfort' or 'consolation'. The people of Judah knew that the prophecy meant the destruction of

Nineveh, which had destroyed Israel and taken many inhabitants of the land captive (722BC).

Several of Nahum's prophecies were not just to the people of Nineveh but were also predicting the future. Nahum 1:12 is one such time when God says:

> This is what the LORD says:
> 'Although they have allies and are numerous,
> they will be destroyed and pass away.
> Although I have afflicted you, Judah,
> I will afflict you no more.'

Or Nahum 1:15, which is like Isaiah 52:7, pointing us to a time when the kingdom of God will be established on the earth. In fact, the apostle Paul uses the imagery of Nahum 1:15 in Romans 10:15 referring to the ministry of the Messiah and His disciples.

> Look, there on the mountains,
> the feet of one who brings good news,
> who proclaims peace!
> Celebrate your festivals, Judah,
> and fulfil your vows.
> No more will the wicked invade you;
> they will be completely destroyed.

*Nah. 1:15*

## The background

The book of Nahum was probably written 700 years before the birth of Christ. It was about one hundred to one hundred and fifty years after Jonah passed on the message of forgiveness to the city of Nineveh. Jonah's message to the people of Nineveh was one of God's mercy. Nahum's message is one of judgment.[1] There is some debate about whether Nahum prophesied in the beginning of the reign of Ahaz (743BC) or whether his prophecies refer to the latter half of the reign of Hezekiah (about 709BC).[2][3] It was probably written at the time of the fall of Nineveh at the hands of the Medes and Babylonians in 612BC.[4] This was after the Assyrian destruction of Thebes in Egypt in approximately 663BC mentioned in Nahum 3:8. If the book was written in Jerusalem (soon after 709BC), Nahum would have witnessed the invasion of Sennacherib and the destruction of his host (2 Kgs 19:35). Sennacherib was the king of Assyria from approximately 705BC to 681BC. Assyria was a kingdom on the middle-Tigris, and it extended its rule over Mesopotamia, Anatolia and Syria-Palestine. The capital of Assyria was Nineveh, one of the richest cities of the ancient world.

The city of Nineveh was a large, complicated complex of town and villages, like London today. It was about thirty miles long and ten miles wide. It was served by one great irrigation system and was protected by a network of fortifications and river defences. The inner city of Nineveh was about three miles long, and one and half miles wide. It was situated at the junction of the Tigris and Khoser rivers, making it an ideal trading centre.

The book of Nahum is found in the Masoretic text, which is considered as the authoritative Hebrew and Aramaic text of the twenty-four books of *Tanakh*. It was copied and passed on by the Masoretic Jews between the seventh and tenth centuries. It is found in this text in the early manuscripts such as the Codex Cairensis of 895AD and the tenth-century Aleppo Codex. There were even fragments from Nahum in the Dead Sea Scrolls

known as scroll 4Q169 or the 'Nahum Commentary'. There
are also versions in the Koine Greek found in the Septuagint,
written in the last few centuries BC. It is the seventh book of the
twelve minor prophets.

All we know about Nahum is that he was probably a native
of Galilee. After the deportation of the ten tribes of Israel, he
lived in Jerusalem. Others think that Nahum lived in Elkosh
on the east bank of the Tigris.

The book itself is like a collection of poems and the use of
language is significant – we'll look at that later, as the words are
more important than the delivery. Nahum's message is clear; he
reminds the people of Nineveh and the Assyrian world of God's
impending judgment, the final destruction of Nineveh. The
book was not a call to repentance for the citizens of Nineveh, as
they had already heard about that from the prophet Jonah. At
that time the people had repented in sackcloth and ashes. They
were now just as bad; in fact, worse than they were before.

Nineveh was a city according to Nahum that was a 'city of
blood, full of lies, full of plunder, never without victims' (Nah.
3:1). As a city, it had robbed and plundered all the neighbouring
nations, as it was strongly fortified on every side and they considered themselves invincible. Within twenty years of Nahum's
prophecy, the Babylonians and Medes armies besieged the city
of Nineveh. Nahum 2:5–8a says:

> Nineveh summons her picked troops,
> yet they stumble on their way.
> They dash to the city wall;
> the protective shield is put in place.
> The river gates are thrown open
> and the palace collapses.
> It is decreed that Nineveh

be exiled and carried away.
Her female slaves moan like doves
and beat on their breasts.
Nineveh is like a pool
whose water is draining away.

A sudden rise in the level of the Tigris river caused a breach in the walls and the invading armies swept into the city, plundering and destroying it. Nahum describes what would happen with its subsequent destruction (2:1–4; 3:1–7).

In Nahum 1:14 we are told:

The LORD has given a command concerning you, Nineveh:
'You will have no descendants to bear your name.
I will destroy the images and idols
that are in the temple of your gods.
I will prepare your grave,
for you are vile.'

And in Nahum 2:13 it says:

'I am against you,'
declares the LORD Almighty.
'I will burn up your chariots in smoke,
and the sword will devour your young lions.
I will leave you no prey on the earth.
The voices of your messengers
will no longer be heard.'

The book of Nahum contains only three chapters and is divided into two distinct parts. These are part one: a poem concerning the greatness of God (Nahum 1:1–15) and part two: detailing the overthrow of Nineveh (Nahum 2:1 – 3:19). The following is a summary of the book:

Chapter 1: God's judgment on Nineveh.

- God's power (vv. 1–7).
- Judgment (vv. 8–15).

Chapter 2: Siege and capture of Nineveh.

- The siege and capture of the city (vv. 1–8).
- The city plundered (vv. 9–13).

Chapter 3: The destruction of the city.

- The cruelty and occult practice in the city (vv. 1–7).
- The final desolation predicted (vv. 8–19).

Nahum's style is almost monotonous in tone. The author O. Palmer Robertson, in his book *The Books of Nahum, Habakkuk, and Zephaniah*,[5] highlights that there is something significant about Nahum's language. Phrases used to depict the desolation of Nineveh, such as 'crack of whips, the clatter of wheels' and the description of horsemen charging (Nah 3:2), highlight the seriousness of Nahum's purpose and message: that Nineveh will be judged for its wickedness. The people of Assyria were so cruel that they would burn the sons and daughters of their enemies, destroying their enemies and disposing of their bodies as rubbish. Dead bodies and heads on spears could be found across the countryside.

These people were ruthless. I am reminded of the fictional Orcs in J.R.R. Tolkien's work *The Lord of the Rings*.[6] These were frightening creatures and foot soldiers bred from men and elves serving the evil master, the Dark Lord of Mordor. For about three years, every Christmas, we would head to the cinema to watch another instalment of the film trilogy. We all agreed that we didn't like the Orcs as they were scary, ruthless beings. This evil is not captured and secured by works of fantasy, but it can be seen in the soldiers of many armies since the Assyrians dominated the Middle East. Not only were they ruthless and evil in character but they were proud of their achievements. The journalist Jonathan Jones describes Assyrian carvings in the British Museum from this time as 'artistic propaganda', which he went on to describe as relishing 'every detail of torture, massacre, battlefield executions and human displacement'.[7]

It was to these people that God had sent Jonah, one hundred to one hundred and fifty years earlier. The theologian and writer Colin Sinclair suggest that Jonah went to Nineveh about 770BC and Nahum spoke to them in 620BC.[8] Again, we need to be reminded that God is a merciful God. In Jonah's time, God forgave the people of Nineveh as they repented, but there is a time when we will face judgment as individuals and as a nation. Generations had passed and still the people did not want to listen to God. Jonah warned the people that now was the time to seek God's forgiveness and Nahum warned them that it was too late!

It is also interesting to note that, although the Assyrian people were pretty brutal, especially around their treatment of their enemies, Nahum's own king was evil too. Nahum was a prophet possibly at the same time as Habakkuk, Zephaniah and Jeremiah. Habakkuk was considered a professional prophet, singer, or even a Levite based at the Temple and speaking into the politics and culture during King Josiah's reign in 640–609BC or at the start of King Jehoiakim's.[9] A contemporary of Jeremiah, he spoke to the people of Judah just before the Babylonian capture of Jerusalem. Jeremiah's ministry was during the reign of King Josiah just before the king called Judah to repentance during 640–609BC. Zephaniah also encouraged King Josiah to make these reforms, turning the nation to face God again.

The first-century Romano-Jewish historian Flavius Josephus suggests that Jotham was king of Judah during Nahum's time, but others suggest that it was during the reign of King Ahaz or even Manasseh. King Jotham was 25 when he came to the throne and reigned Judah for sixteen years. He was a God-fearing king and God blessed his reign.[10] His son Ahaz succeeded Jotham to the throne after he died.

King Ahaz, however, was very different from his father and his story is told in 2 Kings 16 where he is depicted as an evil king. At the start of his reign he was asked to join a coalition: with the northern kingdom of Israel and with Syria to defend themselves against the Assyrians.[11] The prophet Isaiah advised him to put his trust in God, not kings, but Ahaz did not listen. Things did not end well, and Samaria and the northern kingdom were captured. Judah eventually became a sub-servant kingdom to Assyria.

Ahaz trusted idols rather than the one true God, allowing unlawful sacrifices to other gods to take place across the kingdom. During his reign, Judah came under Assyria's suzerainty. What I mean is that it became a tributary state under Assyria's political rule. Hezekiah then followed his father to the throne as the thirteenth king of Judah. Hezekiah was a righteous king and tried to serve God. He saw his fellow countrymen of Israel turn from God. He was proactive in defending his country, rebelling against the Assyrian rule and fortifying Jerusalem, even digging out the Siloam tunnel to bring water to the city from the springs of Gihon.[12] Hezekiah had tried to appease the Assyrian king by ransacking the Temple and paying a ransom.[13] Sennacherib wasn't interested in money, he wanted to capture Jerusalem. Hezekiah turned to Isaiah and Isaiah told him not to worry.

Hezekiah was able to remind his people that they served Yahweh and He would protect them. Isaiah prophesied that Jerusalem would not fall. An article by the *National Geographic* magazine describes Isaiah as the hero of the siege of Jerusalem.[14] The account was found in three artefacts, which details the events of Sennacherib's campaign against Judah. It was discovered in the ruins of Nineveh in 1830. One of the inscribed artefacts is called 'Sennacherib's prism' and tells us of the defeat of forty-six of Judah's cities and mentions that King Hezekiah was in Jerusalem 'like a caged bird'. It tells us the story of the siege of Jerusalem.[15] The Assyrian army were destroyed by God's angel,[16] although some suggest that the army was infected by a plague that decimated them and saved Jerusalem.[17]

Hezekiah is thought to reign between 715–686BC and then his oldest son, Manasseh, came to power. This really was one of the worst times of Judah's history as people turned away from God, and idol worship was the norm. Manasseh was about 12 years old when he came to the throne and reigned for fifty-five years.[18] The Bible describes Manasseh in 2 Kings 21:2: 'He did evil in the eyes of the LORD, following the detestable practices of the nations the LORD had driven out before the Israelites.' Manasseh rebuilt the pagan idols that his father, Hezekiah, had destroyed, even in the Temple in Jerusalem. He practised witchcraft, divinations and liaised with mediums. God spoke through the prophets warning Judah that He would tolerate this behaviour no more.

The people of Judah would have rejoiced to hear that the Assyrian Empire that had kept them suppressed for so many years was to be judged. You would have thought it should have reminded them that they too were to be judged. Again and again God had showed great mercy to his people. There would be a time in the future, however, when Jerusalem would be destroyed.[19]

### More history

The Assyrian captivity occurred when several thousand Jews from Israel and Judah were resettled in Assyria. The northern kingdom was captured by the Neo-Assyrian kings in around 733 or 740BC. This is mentioned in 1 Chronicles 5:26. Twenty years after the initial deportation, Samaria was captured. In 2 Chronicles 30 we are told that King Hezekiah in Judah invited some of the people of the northern kingdom who had escaped exile to join in the Passover feast.

Sargon II and Sennacherib captured Judah some ten years later although Jerusalem was not besieged. He captured some of the fortified cities, but God spared Judah as Sennacherib was murdered by his own sons. Judah was not spared, and during a three-staged approach, King Nebuchadnezzar, king of Babylon, captured Judah. The Babylonian Exile occurred in 586BC when Jerusalem was destroyed. Jeremiah warned Israel that this would happen. The Babylonian King Nebuchadnezzar also warned the Jews that, if they crossed him, he would ruin them as he had devastated Ashkelon, the capital of their enemies, the Philistines. The prophets Jeremiah and Ezekiel mention this. The Temple was plundered by King Nebuchadnezzar. Jesus predicted the destruction of the second Temple in Matthew 24:1–28, Mark 13:1–23 and Luke 21:5–24. The second

Temple was destroyed by the Romans in response to the Jewish revolt. The Temple had only survived roughly 585 years and has never been rebuilt.

Several years ago, I surprised Malcolm with a trip to Jerusalem for his birthday. We had an amazing trip, visiting the places that Jesus walked. It was so moving standing where Gethsemane would have been, across the Kidron Valley on the Mount of Olives. I could just imagine looking towards Jerusalem and thinking about how imposing the Temple would have been. Now the Temple Mount is a holy site for Jewish people, Muslims and Christians, but the Temple has not been rebuilt. The Temple vessels sit ready and are on display off Misgav Ladach Street in the Old City of Jerusalem in the Temple Institute for when the third Temple is built on the foundations of the old one. The Jewish people may be waiting for a time when the Temple is rebuilt and the Messiah returns, but we know God's Son has come. We are reminded through the stories of history that God will judge His people but that He had a clear plan of salvation.

**The main message**

Nahum may have had a clear message to the people of Nineveh, but this same message was as pertinent to his own nation. King David reminds us of God's mercy in Psalm 145:8: 'The LORD is gracious and compassionate, slow to anger and rich in love.' This is the message of Scripture that is repeated again and again. It is one that we need to be reminded about for our own families, for our own nation.

Psalm 103:8–12 says:

> The LORD is compassionate and gracious,
> slow to anger, abounding in love.
> He will not always accuse,
> nor will he harbour his anger for ever;
> he does not treat us as our sins deserve
> or repay us according to our iniquities.
> For as high as the heavens are above the earth,
> so great is his love for those who fear him;
> as far as the east is from the west,
> so far has he removed our transgressions from us.

God is merciful but he is also a God of justice. It is as if we are faced with the two faces of God – both one who is judge and another who is merciful. The journalist Elise Harris wrote an article for the Catholic News Agency in 2016, quoting Pope Francis and his view on mercy and justice. Pope Francis said that rather than contradicting each other, the two go hand in hand: "'Sacred Scripture presents us with God as infinite mercy, but also as perfect justice. How are these two things reconciled? How can the reality of mercy be articulated with the need for justice" . . . While these two characteristics can seem like opposites, "in reality it's not like this, because it's precisely the mercy of God that brings the fulfilment of true justice"[20] God cannot be indifferent to sin but He is also merciful. This is challenging as we turn to Him in prayer. We can even struggle to know what to call Him.

The Jewish people believe that God is both 'Elohim' and 'Adonai'. Elohim is translated as 'God', and is found mainly in the book of Genesis. Elohim is the God of all creation who has all authority and is sovereign of all. God is also a merciful and just God. They are taught to approach God in prayer respecting this duality. There are certainly times when we can almost become blasé about God's forgiveness. We sin and sin again and know we will be forgiven – that's right; God is merciful; that is true – we have forgiveness through Jesus' act of salvation, but we also need to remember that one day there will be a day of judgment even for those who know and believe in Jesus. I have met people who do not believe in the Old Testament God of judgment. The entire Bible, however, from Genesis to Revelation, reveals a God who is the judge of a fractured broken world but also shows mercy to those who repent of their sins and trust in Him.

## About prayer

This is a difficult topic and one that I mulled over for several months. How do we approach God in prayer? How do we communicate to the One who created us, who knows us inside out and can see the scars marring our lives? We turn to Him and He is holy; He looks at us and knows who we are but loves us unconditionally. To understand God's mercy and salvation we also need to understand his judgment and the concept of repentance. How do we pray? Thankfully Jesus taught us how to pray in Matthew 6:9–13:

> Our Father in heaven,
> hallowed be your name,
> your kingdom come,
> your will be done,
> on earth as it is in heaven.
> Give us today our daily bread.
> And forgive us our debts,
> as we also have forgiven our debtors.
> And lead us not into temptation,
> but deliver us from the evil one.

In this prayer, we are asking God to help us live as He wants us to. We are also asking for ongoing forgiveness. For the Christian, this means an ongoing journey of 'turning' or repenting, making a daily decision to live life in obedience to Christ. Interestingly, the meaning of repentance in the Greek is the phrase 'be ye repenting' from the word '*metanoeite*'.[21] Metanoia can be defined as a change in one's way of life as a result of penitence or spiritual conversion. To repent is a decision to live life differently, to live as God would want us to live, rather than how we might want to lead our lives. The people of Nineveh turned to face God but did not keep walking in the right direction. Repentance is also a Roman military phrase meaning 'to turn away'. It is about making a conscious decision to stop doing things your way and follow God. With repentance comes God's mercy.

There are two different attitudes to repentance. The first of these attitudes is attrition, which is sorrow related to a fear of punishment. Judas was repentant for what he had done only in the sense that he wished he hadn't done it. I am thinking of my two golden retrievers, Buzz and Woody, who know when they have done wrong. The other day they stole a packet of biscuits off the worktop. Crumbs and rubbish everywhere. They knew they had done wrong. Their ears turned back, and they slumped in front of me. They may have shown some level of attrition but two days later they stole a packet of crisps.

Judas was sorry for himself; he knew he was opening himself up to punishment and took matters into his own hands, ending his own life.

Contrition is the second attitude that reflects true repentance where the penitent person acknowledges that they have sinned against God. If you are contrite, you understand that you deserve to be punished. The person does not lose hope, however, as they are held up by the hope of forgiveness. This attitude of contrition is seen in in Psalm 51. David recognises that he has offended God. Psalm 51:1–4 says:

> Have mercy on me, O God,
> according to your unfailing love;
> according to your great compassion
> blot out my transgressions.
> Wash away all my iniquity
> and cleanse me from my sin.
>
> For I know my transgressions,
> and my sin is always before me.
> Against you, you only, have I sinned
> and done what is evil in your sight;
> so you are right in your verdict
> and justified when you judge.

Ezekiel 3:17–21 also speaks about repentance:

> Son of man, I have made you a watchman for the people of Israel; so hear the word I speak and give them warning from me. When I say to a wicked person, 'You will surely die,' and you do not warn them or speak out to dissuade them from their evil ways in order to save their life, that wicked person will die for their sin, and I will hold you accountable for their blood. But if you do warn the wicked person and they do not turn from their wickedness or from their evil ways, they will die for their sin; but you will have saved yourself.
>
> Again, when a righteous person turns from their righteousness and does evil, and I put a stumbling-block before them, they will die. Since you did not warn them, they will die for their sin. The

righteous things that person did will not be remembered, and I will hold you accountable for their blood. But if you do warn the righteous person not to sin and they do not sin, they will surely live because they took warning, and you will have saved yourself.

We don't always like the process of repentance, as it can be painful. Instead we can develop a mindset that says that grace covers sins, and it does, but we are omitting repentance. Our prayers should be directed at God our Father, the creator of all things, who can forgive us our sins if we ask Him.

Again and again we have heard that God is willing to forgive. 2 Chronicles 7:14 says: 'if my people, who are called by my name, will humble themselves and pray and seek my face and turn from their wicked ways, then I will hear from heaven, and I will forgive their sin and will heal their land.'

Charles Spurgeon suggests that the Lord's Prayer is a model for prayer, rather than something to be recited word for word. He also suggested that it should be a 'heavenly Pattern for Our Earthly Life'. He recommended that we mention our sins and deal with repentance. Our prayers for our nation can also be based on the Lord's Prayer. This prayer is nestled in the centre of the Sermon on the Mount in the book of Matthew, chapters 5 to 7. If the whole Sermon on the Mount from Matthew was a triangle, then these words would be the base: 'let your will be done on earth as it is in heaven'.[22] 'It is a brave prayer, which only heaven-born faith can utter; yet it is not the offspring of presumption, for presumption never longs for the will of the Lord to be perfectly performed.'[23] And this is not a prayer we say lightly, as not only are we challenged to repentance, but we are praying that our culture and communities will obey God.

The famous theologian and reformer John Calvin from the sixteenth century said:

When we pray that the earth may become obedient to the will of God, it is not necessary that we should look particularly at every individual. It is enough for us to declare, by such a prayer as this, that we hate and regret whatever we perceive to be contrary to the will of God, and long for its utter destruction, not only that it may be the rule of all our affections, but that we may yield ourselves without reserve, and with all cheerfulness, to its fulfilment.[24]

A tough prayer, as it may mean that the nation is warned to repent just as in Jonah's time, and then one day they will receive a final warning like Nahum's message.

## Let's pray

We may read people's prayers and they can help us when we don't have the words to say. There are times when we just don't know how to start. The best thing we can do is use the words of Jesus. He taught us how to pray.

Our Father in heaven,
Show us what you are like. We want to know You better.
We also plead for the world. There are so many things going wrong, and we need Your help.
You alone know what is best for our world.
Feed us with what we need for physical, mental and spiritual strength.
Help us to forgive others like You have forgiven us.
And keep us safe from harm's way.
Protect us from the evil one.
We know we can trust You.
We shout praise to Your name.
Amen.

# 5
## Micah

# A Cry for Justice and Mercy

The message of Micah contains some serious warnings for the people of Israel, but it is also a message of hope. It is such a mixture of messages from doom and despair to deliverance and peace. His prophecies cover the full spectrum from dire warnings to joyful reconciliation.

Sometimes I watch the news or social media and am embarrassed by what Christians say. They are very outspoken on all manner of issues, from books children should not read to TV programmes. They have a right to stand up and say things, but they are often remembered for what they stand against rather than what they stand for. We hear of people protesting about abortion and same-sex relationships, greed and addiction. How often do we hear them shouting about mercy, justice, or a fair society for everyone?

For me, this book is like a banner in one of the picket lines or outside a church building. It stands up and shouts these things. I am reminded that I too can plead and petition God and intercede for my own nation that its people will know the One who loves them.

**The main character**

Micah prophesied during the time of Isaiah, Hosea and Amos. Isaiah was probably a prince in the royal court. Micah was a rural saint, a man brought up in the hill country of Israel. His call is remarkably similar to theirs, during a time of injustice. Through tears, Micah calls for a society governed by God's principles of justice and mercy. This follows on from what we learned earlier about Amos. We look at how justice and mercy appear in our own lives.

Micah is the sixth of the twelve minor prophets in the Hebrew Bible. His book sits between the books Jonah and Nahum in our Bibles. His name is Mikayahu in Hebrew, which means: 'Who is like Yahweh?' We are told that he was a prophet from the village of Moresheth in Judah.[1] His ministry extended over three kings of Judah and he prophesied to the northern and southern kingdoms of Israel. These were King Jotham, Ahaz and Hezekiah of Judah. Although King Jotham of Judah (750 to 735BC) 'did what was right in the eyes of the LORD' (2 Kgs 15:34), he allowed idolatry to dominate the landscape.[2] His people continued sacrificing and burning incense there. King Ahaz (Assyrian Jehoahaz) was then king of Judah (735–720BC) but became an Assyrian vassal, as he didn't listen to Isaiah's warnings of what would happen if he didn't follow God and trust Him.[3]

Living during these times would have shaken any God-fearing Hebrew. The political landscape was shifting incredibly fast. Anything could happen. All the people had to hang onto God's promise that He was their God. That is what King Hezekiah did (715 and 686BC). He is considered a very righteous king and is even mentioned in the genealogy of Jesus in the Gospel of Matthew.[4] Some consider Micah 6 and 7 to be written during the reign of wicked King Manasseh.[5] Ultimately, Israel failed to listen to Micah, so in 722/721 they were conquered by the Assyrians. In Judah, for the time being, the people flourished as Hezekiah put God first.

Although we do not know a lot about Micah, his ministry was recorded and remembered. Micah is mentioned in the book of Jeremiah, during Jeremiah's trial. The elders of Judah mention Micah and his prophetic message of judgment to remind the leaders of Judah that Jeremiah, just like Micah, had preached about the pending destruction of Jerusalem.

> Some of the elders of the land stepped forward and said to the entire assembly of people, 'Micah of Moresheth prophesied in the days of Hezekiah king of Judah. He told all the people of Judah, "This is what the LORD Almighty says:
>
> "'Zion will be ploughed like a field,
>
> Jerusalem will become a heap of rubble,
>
> the temple hill a mound overgrown with thickets.'"
>
> *Jer. 26:17,18*

Micah and Jeremiah's lives were consequently both spared. Micah and Jeremiah's messages were possibly one of the factors that prompted Hezekiah to initiate his religious reforms at the heart of Judah. Both prophets spoke out the truth they believed God had given them, no matter the cost. On this occasion they were spared. This was not the case for the prophet Zechariah, who was murdered in the Temple.

In Micah's oracles he is clear what his calling is: to call out sin and to highlight injustice. In Micah 3:8 he says:

> But as for me, I am filled with power,
>
> with the Spirit of the LORD,

and with justice and might,
to declare to Jacob his transgression,
to Israel his sin.

Micah identifies himself with the poor and the oppressed people of Judah, calling them 'my people'.[6] Some scholars believe that Micah was a poor farmer who keenly felt this oppression, living in it. In fact, Bruce Malchow, throughout his book about social justice in the Hebrew Bible, calls Micah, 'The Rural Prophet.'[7] Dr Claude Mariottini, Professor of Old Testament at the Northern Baptist Seminary calls Micah, 'the prophet of the poor' in his blog post about the prophet.[8] He points out that Micah's birthplace was probably a small rural village or hamlet about twenty-five miles south-west of the major city of Jerusalem. The writer and speaker Charles R. Swindoll suggests that 'It is doubtful that the poor peasants of Judah ever had a stronger champion than their countryman Micah, the powerful preacher'.[9] He may not be of royal lineage like Isaiah, or had his education, or be as popular as Hosea, but he defended the downtrodden with passion. He was sympathetic to the poor and raged at the rich who abused their power.

Micah's home village of Moresheth, as well as Lachish, Judah's second largest city, bordered the Philistines' coast area. When the Assyrians attacked Judah in 701BC they used this route. Micah must have been impacted by it all.


### The background

The book is considered to have three main parts which all start with the word 'hear' or 'listen'. These are Micah chapters 1,2, 3 – 5 and 6,7.

In Micah 1 and 2 we read his stark message, warning of imminent judgment to the nations. This is found in in Micah 1:1; 2:2–11; 2:12,13. His book is also a reminder of that judgment to the leaders, see chapter 3. In chapters 4 and 5 we are promised restoration and we can read that in Micah 4:1–5; 5:1–15. In chapters 6 and 7 it looks closely at what repentance looks like today. Micah looks forward to a world at peace under the leadership of a new Davidic monarch or Messiah. Within each section there are a series of alternating oracles of judgment and promises of restoration. God judges but God restores, God judges but God restores. It ends with a reminder that: 'You will again have compassion on us; you will tread our sins underfoot and hurl all our iniquities into the depths of the sea' (Mic. 7:19).

In Micah 1:3–7 God's judgment is pronounced over Samaria. The culture was one of false worship, fraud and deception, sexual immorality, bribery and worship of the occult. These practices have reached the gates of God's people in the city of Jerusalem. This is a real reminder to followers of the one true God that they are to be holy as God is holy.

Leviticus 11:44 says:

I am the LORD your God; consecrate yourselves and be holy, because I am holy. Do not make yourselves unclean by any creature that moves along the ground.

We see what life without God can be like and what God expects of us. Evil-doers plot their wicked plans; God plots their judgment. In chapter 2 Micah laments over the wealthy classes that are unjust. They have coveted fields and land and oppressed the ordinary homeowners. They think nothing will touch them and walk through the streets proud of what they have done.

Maybe it is because I have Scottish heritage, but when I read these verses, I am reminded of the 150 years of Highland clearances, when wealthy landowners claimed back their lands in a ruthless way. From 1792 onwards, tenant farmers were evicted from their homes across the Scottish Highlands to make way for sheep farming. Sir John Sinclair had wanted to improve the income from his Langwell estate in Caithness, Scotland. He introduced lucrative sheep farming and evicted the tenant farmers to Badbea, a high clifftop village south of Berriedale. This can be such a dangerous area that the steep Berriedale braes (hillsides) have a graveyard at the start and end of them on the A9 between Helmdale and Lybster. Twelve families were evicted, and eighty people were moved to the clifftop village. The place was so inhospitable that the residents had to tether their animals and small children to avoid them being swept over the cliff edge by the high winds.

Badbea is now the haunting site of the abandoned settlement. There is a memorial at the village which tells the story of the old inhabitants. On visiting my parents a few years ago, Malcolm and I took the family to visit the site. We were constantly shouting at our four children to stay close. It was a harrowing place. Haughty landowners walked through their estates as children were tied to ropes to stop them falling over cliffs. God sees. He hears the voice of the oppressed and the poor. He knows.

**The main message**

Micah's message essentially condemns the oppression of the poor, the political corruption of the leaders of Judah, and the corrupt religious life that occurred during the reign of King

Ahaz. Thus, many scholars believe that Micah's message was one of the factors that prompted Hezekiah to initiate the religious reforms that removed some of the pagan practices that had been introduced into the religious life of Judah.

The book itself is quite short compared to some of the other Old Testament books, but it certainly packs a punch! It includes lament (1:8–16, 7:8–10), words from God (2:3,4), songs and prayers of petition and praise (7:14–20) and a 'covenant lawsuit' in which Micah informs the people that God is suing Israel for breach of contract of the Mosaic covenant (see Mic. 6:1–5). The theologian Willem VanGemeren discusses this type of prophetic word in his book, *Interpreting the Prophetic Word*.[10] He suggests that much like a marriage contract, the Mosaic covenant required the Israelites to be faithful to God as outlined in the book of Deuteronomy in Micah chapter 6. Micah describes God taking his covenant partner Judah to court for breaking this covenant. This is as bad as it gets. Hosea also provides us with this picture of a lawsuit in chapter 4 of Hosea.

Some of the prophecies of Micah are also quoted in the New Testament. See Matthew 2:1–6:

> After Jesus was born in Bethlehem in Judea, during the time of King Herod, Magi from the east came to Jerusalem and asked, 'Where is the one who has been born king of the Jews? We saw his star when it rose and have come to worship him.'
>
> When King Herod heard this he was disturbed, and all Jerusalem with him. When he had called together all the people's chief priests and teachers of the law, he asked them where the Messiah was to be born. 'In Bethlehem in Judea,' they replied, 'for this is what the prophet has written:

'"But you, Bethlehem, in the land of Judah,
are by no means least among the rulers of Judah;
for out of you will come a ruler
who will shepherd my people Israel."'

In Matthew 10:35,36 Jesus quoted Micah 7:6:

For I have come to turn
'a man against his father,
a daughter against her mother,
a daughter-in-law against her mother-in-law –
a man's enemies will be the members of his own household.'

Micah 7:20 is also quoted by Jesus' relative Zechariah, in his song in Luke 1:72–73: 'to show mercy to our ancestors and to remember his holy covenant, the oath he swore to our father Abraham . . .'

## About prayer

We heard a lot about justice in chapter 2 of this book, when we heard about Amos. It is still difficult, isn't it? The question I often come back to is: How do I pray for justice? It is a little like those adverts on the TV trying to make you feel guilty so you will support hungry people in Africa. There is usually a famous person delivering a voice-over picture of starving children. I switch off. Perhaps it is because I hear it too often, or because it feels such a huge problem, that I do not know what to do. Our concern to pray about justice issues should not come from guilt but for a heart like Micah's.

Throughout the book of Micah, we have learned that God has a heart for justice. Care for those oppressed, widowed, orphaned and poor is the very heartbeat of this book. We can almost touch Micah's passion. Sometimes we just do not know where to begin.

We can start by talking to God. Prayer is essential to justice. In an article on the World Prayer Centre website written by Natasha Ruddock,[11] she reminds us that there are more than 40 million people trapped in slavery today, one in four of which are children. Estimates for slavery in the UK is approximately 136,000 but this could be higher.

Natasha suggests we do the following when we pray:

- Focus on God's character.
- Remember that God hears our cries and petitions.
- We know that God promises to answer our prayers
- We may feel burdened by these needs so we need to hand them to God.
- We need to persevere in praying.

These are just examples of what we can do. They are little steps that can make a difference. The biggest step we can take is to ask God to give us a heart like his. If our lives begin to beat close to God's rhythm, then we begin to pray spontaneous prayers that incorporate God's justice; worship Him, incorporating themes of thanksgiving for justice and mercy; and plead for the widow, the refugee or the orphan.

Micah is a short, sharp book that penetrates our conscience and reminds us to pray! To the people of the day there is a strong theme of restoration that runs through – a little like the words through a stick of rock. There are dire warnings and threats of punishment. There is also an encouraging and reassuring message of future hope: peace, not just for Judah, but for all peoples and nations.

**Let's pray**

Father God,

You created us in Your own image and likeness. We have turned our back on You and allowed sin to change what we do. For this we are sorry.

Throughout the world there is much injustice – we do not care about the rights of other people. There is much injustice and corruption taking place in our world today. This is not just in our own lives but also in the lives that govern us.

Lord, we pray, right all the wrongs that are taking place in our world. Vindicate those that are being treated unjustly. Teach us to seek justice, to defend the oppressed, to support the fatherless and the plea of the widow.

Lord, in Your grace and mercy, hear our prayer.

In the precious name of the Lord Jesus.

Amen.

# 6
## Zephaniah

# A Plea to God

They always say that the best things, or good things, come in small packages. I think we could say that of Zephaniah. It is a short book of three chapters that is found in our Bible between the books of Habakkuk and the book of Haggai. Zephaniah is one of the minor prophets who prophesied in the seventh century BC in the days of Josiah, king of Judah (640–609BC). He is ninth in the literary order of the minor prophets. He lived and prophesied in the days of Josiah, king of Judah before his reforms in 621BC, before the captivity. He was a contemporary of Jeremiah. It is commonly thought that Zephaniah prophesied approximately thirty years before Habakkuk although we find the books in a different order in our Bibles.[1] Again, the focus of the book is challenging the people about their wickedness. Under the reign of the kings Amon and Manasseh of Judah, idol worship was common practice. The cults of Baal and Astarte prospered, particularly in Jerusalem. Later, we hear that Josiah became a dedicated reformer, as he wanted to end idolatry and the abuse of the holy places.[2] Josiah reformed the Temple, which had fallen into a state of neglect, and established the importance of the law. Zephaniah's writing provides us with a clearer understanding of Josiah's reforms.

## The main character

We are told at the start of the book that Zephaniah was a man who had a big calling. He was to be God's voice to a corrupt and godless nation. They were caught up in sexual immorality, idolatry, pagan fertility rites, astrology and a real indifference to their God. But despite that, they were God's chosen nation. Zephaniah's name can be translated from the Greek as 'Yahweh has concealed' or 'the one whom Yahweh has hidden'. Zephaniah tells us that his father was Cushi and was around during the time of Amon, the son of Manasseh. Both were wicked kings in Judah. Perhaps he does this to remind us that you can serve God no matter what your background is. Hebrew tradition was that one would mention one's father as a point of honour. I am Deborah (Debbie), daughter of Kenneth Hunter, Christian and retired pastor. Here we see that Zephaniah was from a royal line, but his father's name is not something to sing about. Would you want to celebrate that you were related to the Kray twins or Ted Bundy?

Zephaniah goes all the way back to Hezekiah. This is probably because the prophet wanted to highlight that he was a descendant of one of Judah's good kings too. All we can guess is that Zephaniah mentions not only his father and grandfather, but also his great-grandfather and his great-great-grandfather because they were not prophets. Prophets were usually descended from prophets. Zephaniah did not have the pedigree of a prophet, but God still spoke to and through him. I have no doubt that, as a young man, he would have been surrounded by the trappings of idolatry, and wealth, child sacrifice and unjust killing – and bad influences on a young mind.[3]

## The background

On initial reviewing of the words, we may think that Zephaniah appears to be as poetic as the other minor prophets. There is, however, some debate about the way he arranges them.[4] In normal Hebrew poetry there are parallelisms, which are a prominent feature in Hebrew poetry. This parallelism is also commonly seen in the book of Proverbs, or the Psalms. The words of two or more lines of the text are causally related in some way. It is a rhetorical device that groups together words or phrases of equivalent meanings, so that they create a definite pattern. It therefore gives the writing a sense of balance. The Bible scholar and Oxford professor of poetry Robert Lowth suggests that the poetry sections are 'altogether prosaic'.[5] Lowth's writings show us that he was probably the first modern Bible scholar to draw attention to the poetic structure of Zephaniah and the other books.[6] Many of the great reformers, such as Luther and Calvin, highlight the historicity rather than the language.[7] Whether it is more like poetry or prose, the meaning of the words stands out.

## The main message

Reading the book of Zephaniah, you can almost hear him preaching his message. He starts with a public exhortation to repentance. He then reminds the people that God promises His protection for Judah although not for the neighbouring nations – a reminder of God's covenant with Abraham and his descendants. In the final section, the prophet focuses on the sins of Jerusalem but also encourages his listeners, referring to God's future blessings. The book is mainly historical, interspersed with Zephaniah's own poetic style.

Chapter 1:2,3: in this section we hear the warnings about future judgment. This would be a time when God's judgment would descend on Judah and Jerusalem as a punishment for their behaviour. This judgment was for everyone (1:7–13) and it would be catastrophic (1:14–18). Zephaniah describes the people as people who enjoyed 'violence and deceit' (1:9). They were blasé about God (1:12) and focused on materialism and pleasures (1:13). It really does not sound that much different from the society we live in today.

The phrase, 'The day of the LORD' appears seven times in Zephaniah. The 'day of the LORD' is a biblical term and is described as, 'The sun will be turned to darkness and the moon to blood before the coming of the great and dreadful day of the LORD' (Joel 2:31). It is also mentioned in Acts 2:20. You can be forgiven for thinking that it just refers to temporal events such as the invasion by a foreign army or a besieged city. In many of the prophetic texts, the 'day of the LORD' will mean destruction and judgment for all people. In Zephaniah 1:8 the 'day of the LORD' is also thought to be about Jesus' death and sacrifice:

> On the day of the LORD's sacrifice
> I will punish the officials
> and the king's sons
> and all those clad
> in foreign clothes.

During Zephaniah's time, the people living in Judah turned the worship of God into a fiasco. They built their own places of worship to serve idols and desecrated the Temple. Again, not that different from today, when as a nation we can make a mockery of worship, particularly when we live in open sin. Zephaniah reminds us how seriously God takes our lives and relationship with Him. And if we have failed Him – there is forgiveness in His Son.

In chapter 2:4–15 we hear that this message is not only for the people of Jerusalem but that the entire world is subject to judgment. It includes the Philistines (vv. 4–7) Moabites, Ammonites (vv. 8–11), Ethiopians (v. 12), Assyrians and those living in Nineveh (vv. 13–15).

In Zephaniah 3:1–7: again, the prophet focuses on Jerusalem:

> Woe to the city of oppressors,
> rebellious and defiled!
> She obeys no one,
> she accepts no correction.
> She does not trust in the LORD,
> she does not draw near to her God.
> Her officials within her
> are roaring lions;
> her rulers are evening wolves,
> who leave nothing for the morning.
> Her prophets are unprincipled;
> they are treacherous people.
> Her priests profane the sanctuary
> and do violence to the law.
> The Lord within her is righteous;
> he does no wrong.
> Morning by morning he dispenses his justice,
> and every new day he does not fail,
> yet the unrighteous know no shame.
> 'I have destroyed nations;

their strongholds are demolished.
I have left their streets deserted,
with no one passing through.
Their cities are laid waste;
they are deserted and empty.
Of Jerusalem I thought,
"Surely you will fear me
and accept correction!"'

In Zephaniah 3:9–20 there is a shift of vision and Zephaniah mentions the kingdom of God. This is Zephaniah 3:14,15:

Sing, Daughter Zion;
shout aloud, Israel!
Be glad and rejoice with all your heart,
Daughter Jerusalem!
The LORD has taken away your punishment,
he has turned back your enemy.
The LORD, the King of Israel, is with you;
never again will you fear any harm.

Zephaniah's message contains three major doctrines:

- God is sovereign. He is holy.
- One day there will be judgment.
- God offers hope to those who repent and trust in Him.

**About prayer**

Zephaniah reminds us that God is holy and that we should not take this for granted. I think there are times when I focus so much on the love of God that I forget that he is a holy God. The other day I was driving to work about 7.30 a.m. and feeling a little bruised. It had been a tough week resulting in some unfounded accusations. I was frustrated by it all and felt it was also unjust. As I was driving along, my car was suddenly filled with light as the sun's rays almost exploded in my car. It was not an ordinary sunrise. I felt overcome with the remembrance of the sovereignty of God. I had to pull the car over and gain emotional control. I even had to try to fix my blotchy mascara! I think that God's sovereignty and His holiness are intertwined.

The American theologian R.C. Sproul says of holiness: 'The primary meaning of holy is "separate." It comes from an ancient word that meant, "to cut," or "to separate." Perhaps even more accurate would be the phrase "a cut above something." When we find a garment or another piece of merchandise that is outstanding, that has a superior excellence, we use the expression that it is "a cut above the rest."'[8] The Bible paints us a picture of a God who is transcendentally separate as He is so far above and beyond us that He can at times seem almost foreign to us. Exodus 15:11 says:

> Who among the gods
> is like you, Lord?
> Who is like you –
> majestic in holiness,
> awesome in glory,
> working wonders?

And we are commanded to be holy as God is holy in Leviticus 10:3.

Moses said to Aaron, 'This is what God meant when he said,
To the one who comes near me,
I will show myself holy;
Before all the people,
I will show my glory.'

*MSG*

A tall order and one that we cannot achieve without God's intervention. I don't know about you, but I feel I constantly fail God and never feel good enough. I know that I would never have been able to live under the law without failing him. I would never be able to have a relationship with God based on my self-righteousness or good works. Living under the law means that we are justified by works, obeying the Mosaic Law.[9] You need to be willing to see your true reflection in the mirror to clearly see that you cannot attain true holiness. The Scottish preacher Andrew Murray said, 'The greatest test of whether the holiness we profess to seek or to attain is truth and life will be whether it produces an increasing humility in us. In man, humility is the one thing needed to allow God's holiness to dwell in him and shine through him. The chief mark of counterfeit holiness is lack of humility. The holiest will be the humblest.' In other words, we need to be humble before a holy God, seeking his life-saving forgiveness through His Son. We may look in the mirror and see who we really are; God looks at us and sees the reflection of His Son in us.

I think we also need to know who God is before we try to be like Him. The people in the time of Zephaniah did not try to do so until Josiah, king of Judah, implemented his reforms during his reign of 640-609BC. Josiah ordered the high priest,

Hilkiah, to use the money from taxes to renovate the Temple. During the renovation of the Temple they discovered a scroll of 'the Book of the Law' (2 Kgs 22) which was possibly a copy of part of the book of Deuteronomy.[10] This deeply impacted Josiah and he purged the Temple of all foreign idols, dedicating it to the worship of Yahweh. He had come to know the one and only true God.

I think we need to be reminded at times of God's holiness. That is what happened to Isaiah when he had a dramatic revelation. In Isaiah 6:1–7 we are told:

In the year that King Uzziah died, I saw the Lord, high and exalted, seated on a throne; and the train of his robe filled the temple. Above him were seraphim, each with six wings: with two wings they covered their faces, with two they covered their feet, and with two they were flying. And they were calling to one another:

'Holy, holy, holy is the LORD Almighty;
the whole earth is full of his glory.'

At the sound of their voices the doorposts and thresholds shook and the temple was filled with smoke.

'Woe to me!' I cried. 'I am ruined! For I am a man of unclean lips, and I live among a people of unclean lips, and my eyes have seen the King, the LORD Almighty.'

Then one of the seraphim flew to me with a live coal in his hand, which he had taken with tongs from the altar.[7] With it he touched my mouth and said, 'See, this has touched your lips; your guilt is taken away and your sin atoned for.'

Isaiah's response was that he confessed his own ungodliness and that of his people. The book of Zephaniah reminds us that God is holy. That revelation should hopefully move our hearts and souls as it did for Isaiah. When I was sat in my car, I sobbed as I was reminded that God is holy, that I get things wrong. As we pray to God our Father, it is good to remember that He is also our creator. He is a Holy God.

I came to know who Jesus was through the teaching in Sunday school and through the work of Scripture Union in my local secondary school. I was 14 years old. My journey to my secondary school involved a tiring walk down a long road, a five-mile minibus journey to our nearest village and a longer bus journey to Thurso High School in Thurso, northern Scotland. A couple of times a month I used to get off the first bus on the way home and visit a couple of the older ladies from our church. I really loved them. I felt that they were in some extraordinary way related to me. I always remember a profound conversation I had with one of them as I discussed how I was struggling with doing what I did not want to do and so failing Jesus. She advised me to read Romans 7:15: 'I do not understand what I do. For what I want to do I do not do, but what I hate I do.'

She told me I was in good company – that even the apostle Paul struggled with it. Then she quoted Charles Spurgeon, who is said to have stated: 'I believe the holier a man becomes, the more he mourns over the unholiness which remains in him.'[11] The closer you get to Jesus, the more you see you must change. His light shines through our cracked vessels.

Spurgeon also is reported to have said: 'I have now concentrated all my prayers into one and that one prayer is this – that I may die to self – and live wholly to Him.'[12] A grasp of the holiness of God should change our attitude and action in prayer and worship. My prayers change from knowing how much I have failed God to seeing what Jesus has done for me.

I love the old hymn, 'I Stand Amazed in the Presence' by Charles Hutchinson Gabriel (1856–1932).

> I stand amazed in the presence
> Of Jesus the Nazarene,
> And wonder how He could love me,
> A sinner condemned, unclean.
>
> How marvelous! How wonderful!
> And my song shall ever be:
> How marvelous! How wonderful!
> Is my Savior's love for me![13]

Charles Hutchinson Gabriel also used the pseudonyms of Charlotte G. Homer, H.A. Henry, and S.B. Jackson in the printing and publication of his songs! I am unsure why this is the case, but it is estimated that he wrote and composed between 7,000 and 8,000 songs under these names, many of which are still sung today. He had a poor home life as he was born in a shanty town in Iowa in 1856. He would often sing hymns to the European and local settlers with his father. He edited forty-three song books, seven men's chorus books, nineteen anthem collections and twenty-three cantatas. This is my favourite hymn.

We are not living in the days of the minor prophets when worship was regulated by the priests. We don't need someone to pray on our behalf although Jesus intercedes with His Father for us (Rom. 8:34). We do need to be reminded that in prayer and worship we need to take the holiness of God seriously. God does not want our half-hearted response. That is irreverent. The idea of reverence for God may have started in the Old Testament but it is something that we still need to consider. God taught the Israelites how to show proper reverence to Him in the laws outlined in the book of Deuteronomy. We didn't know how to worship a holy God, so He spelled it out for us. He gave us His law and allowed His Son to die for us so we can have a relationship with Him. Let the knowledge of His holiness and sovereignty undo you, but also allow Him to piece you together bit by bit. This knowledge will challenge our complacency, stamp on our irrelevance and help us to remain focused on Him.

### Love and justice

I think you can finish reading Zephaniah and think the focus is on judgment, missing out that it also speaks of love. If John 3:16 sums up the message of salvation in the Gospels, then Zephaniah 3:17 is this message in the books of the minor prophets. Certainly, this book contains some of the most vivid images of God's justice and love found in any of the prophetic books. God is just and He also has a heart for rescuing His world from evil. Bonded together, God's justice and love give us a future and a hope:

> The LORD your God is with you,
> the Mighty Warrior who saves.
> He will take great delight in you;
> in his love he will no longer rebuke you,
> but will rejoice over you with singing.

*Zeph. 3:17*

Zephaniah acknowledges that God is sovereign. He reminds us that God judges Judah, the surrounding countries and the whole earth. Zephaniah had the courage to challenge his nation. Israel had allowed itself to be influenced by the nations around it. He had confidence in what he was saying. His book starts with the words, 'The word of the LORD' and ends with 'says the LORD.' There is also a promise for Israel, a time when their Messiah will come.

The global message of Zephaniah is the clear message that there will be a day of judgment. The 'day of the LORD' will come. Surely, if nothing else, this will shape and sculpture our prayer lives as we fall before our sovereign God, our creator, and ask Him to forgive us. I know I don't spend enough time praying for forgiveness for what I have done and praying for change in my community, my nation. When God, however, shines His light on me, on my complacency, even in the front seat of a Volkswagen Polo, I don't want to rush away.

This book has taught me to intentionally seek God more, for help to become more like Jesus. To persist in praying for my hometown, home county and country. Our culture may reflect Zephaniah's – people who enjoyed violence and deceit, who are blasé about God and are focused on materialism and pleasures – but I am not going to give up praying for change.

**Let's pray**

Almighty God,
Sometimes we look at the world around us and it looks as though the whole world is going mad. There seems to be such a culture of excess in every area of life. Help us to be grateful for what we have. Help us to be good stewards of what You give us.
Through Jesus Christ, our Lord.
Amen.

# 7
# Habakkuk

# Praise and Lament

Like many of the minor prophets, Habakkuk lived during a turbulent time in Israel's history. Life wasn't all plain sailing for God's chosen people. That is like the road map we all seem to travel – plenty of steep curves, unexpected dips and a few hills. If we are honest, often God seems far away, and He does not always answer when we call. Bad things happen to good people and we don't understand why. How should we as Christians and the community of faith respond when our lived experience can be quite different to our faith-filled message? God brings peace but we are anxious, He is always with us, but we don't feel like He is; or God heals, but people catch Covid-19 and die.

Habakkuk points us to praise – to proclaim the truth of God's character and to recount His past faithfulness during times of suffering and difficulty.

The lives of the minor prophets have certainly echoed this kind of response to adversity, where praise becomes an act of faith. We can also be incredibly open and honest about how we are feeling. Living through adversity does not mean we cannot cry out directly to God for help. Habakkuk teaches us about this type of open and honest communication with God.

**The main character**

Habakkuk possibly lived in Judah in 640–609BC during the time of Jeremiah and Nahum. Like many of the minor prophets, there is some debate about when Habakkuk prophesied. He certainly speaks of God raising up the Babylonians in Habakkuk 1:6. Some suggest that he wrote during the twenty-five-year period between the time when Babylon conquered Nineveh and the Assyrian Empire, and the time when Babylon conquered Jerusalem in about 587BC. This was during a time when only the kingdom of Judah remained. This period was at the end of King Josiah's reign.

After Josiah's death, Jehoahaz was proclaimed king. He was the younger brother and was a popular young man. His reign, however, lasted only three months, as he was captured by the Egyptian pharaoh Necho II. Then King Eliakim, or Jehoiakim, as he became known, took the throne as a puppet king for the Egyptians.

After the Egyptians were defeated by the Babylonians at the battle of Carchemish in 605BC, King Nebuchadnezzar II besieged Jerusalem. To save his country and his throne, Jehoiakim changed allegiances and paid heavy tributes from the treasury. He only reigned for eleven years, until 598BC, when he was succeeded by his son Jehoiachin who reigned for only three months.

This was a turbulent time of change and godlessness in Judah's history. Jehoiakim himself was described as a godless tyrant. He is also reported as having incestuous relations with his mother, daughter-in-law and stepmother and to have murdered the husbands of wives he wanted. Jeremiah criticised the king's lifestyle and pleaded with him to repent. Uriah ben

Shemaiah also pleaded with the king to repent and Jehoiakim ordered his execution.[1]

Jehoiakim continued to reign for three years as a puppet king for the Babylonians until the failure of an invasion of Egypt in 601BC. Jehoiakim then switched allegiance back to the Egyptians. You get the impression he was just trying to save this kingdom and his throne. Then in late 598BC, the Babylonian king Nebuchadnezzar II invaded Judah and again laid siege to Jerusalem, which lasted three months. Jehoiakim died before the siege ended, all his plans in ruins. What a tragic time for the king and his family. He was succeeded by his son Jehoiachin, but Jehoiachin was disposed of by King Nebuchadnezzar after only three months. Zedekiah, Jehoiakim's younger brother, then became king, and most of the population of Judah were exiled to Babylon. This was a tragic time for Jehoiakim and all that followed after him.

Scholars are not even certain about the origin of Habakkuk's name. There is debate that his name comes from the Hebrew root word for a plant or the word 'embrace', which was a common root word in seventh-century Judah. It is also thought that his name comes from the word 'wrestle' which appears to be more appropriate although I am not sure if that is right. Habakkuk was wrestling with a difficult issue: if God is good, then why is there evil in the world?

The book consists of five oracles about the Chaldeans, also known as the Babylonians, and Habbakuk is considered a contemporary of Jeremiah and Zephaniah. He is lamenting over what he sees during uncertain times. His questions mirror those of Job as he shares his doubts and fears with God. Habakkuk lived in Judah in 640–609BC during the time of Jeremiah and Nahum.

Warren Wiersbe entitles his book on Habakkuk *From Worry to Worship*[2], as this is exactly what Habakkuk did. He begins worrying about the world around him and God's inaction; he ends the book by worshipping God.

## The background

The book of Habakkuk is the eighth book of the minor prophets. It is interesting, as for most of the other prophets we are told some background information about them such as where they are from or who their father was. All we know about Habakkuk is that he lived in Jerusalem in Judah. In fact, his name is only mentioned in the Bible in Habakkuk 1:1 and Habakkuk 3:1. Habakkuk does, however, appear in the part of the Apocrypha called 'Bel and the Dragon'. This is an additional chapter of the book of Daniel: chapter 14. Although it was included into the canon of Scripture by the Catholic and Orthodox Christians, it is not typically found in modern Bibles today. Certainly, what we do know is that Pesher Habakkuk is a relatively complete scroll and one of the seven original Dead Sea Scrolls discovered in the caves of Qumran in 1947. It was found to contain the first two chapters of the book of the prophet Habakkuk.

The final chapter of this book is also a song, so it is suggested that he was a member of the tribe of Levi. The tribe of Levi had particular religious duties, including working as musicians in the Temple and political responsibilities. The Levites who were not involved in politics played music in the Temple or served as guards. Other notable descendants of the Levite line include Moses, Aaron, Miriam, Samuel, Ezekiel, Ezra and Malachi.

## The main message

Habakkuk is such an important book, as it provides us with an extended public dialogue between Habakkuk and God in chapters 1 and 2. In chapter 1 it sounds as if Habakkuk is despairing because of the evil around him. We are listening in to their conversation. Habakkuk starts the conversation as he is distressed about God's inaction in the world and wants God to act. Rather than run away like Jonah, Habakkuk takes his frustration to God in prayer. Habakkuk poses some difficult questions to God, such as, why is wickedness prospering?

In chapter 1:1–4 he asks, 'Why don't you do something?'

God answers back, 'I will deal with this wickedness through the Chaldeans.'

Then in chapter 1:12 Habakkuk lays out his second complaint: 'You can't use them! They are less righteous than us and we are your chosen people.'

God answers, 'I can use them to judge Judah but I will also judge them.'

Habakkuk's complaint is in chapter 1 verses 2 onwards:

> How long, LORD, must I call for help,
> but you do not listen?
> Or cry out to you, 'Violence!'
> but you do not save?

He was wondering why evil seemed to be winning. In chapter 2, God answers Habakkuk's question. He reminds His people that they can trust in Him, and those people who thought they would get away with their evil would be punished. In chapter three Habakkuk gives God the glory and praise for answering his questions. In Habakkuk 3:2 he says:

> LORD, I have heard of your fame;
> I stand in awe of your deeds, LORD.
> Repeat them in our day,
> in our time make them known;
> in wrath remember mercy.

God's answer to any one of us who asks these questions is that He knows the end from the beginning. He has read the back of the book. We can trust God even when things seem confusing and messy. We can ask God these questions. We can pray to our Father and be honest before Him.

Habakkuk 2:14 says: 'For the earth will be filled with the knowledge of the glory of the LORD as the waters cover the sea.'

## About prayer
### Praise

We travel the range of emotions from lament to praise in such a short time. In chapter 1 we hear Habakkuk's lament, and in chapter 3, Habakkuk praises God, as he now understands and offers a prayer of praise because God is in control.

- He pleads for mercy
- He is afraid of what judgment will look like
- He praises God – for His majesty and power
- He promises to trust God

In Habakkuk 3:3–15 we read two poems (vv. 3–7; vv. 8–15) that tell us of God's deliverance of His people from the Egyptians to their entrance into the Promised Land. The psalm in Habakkuk 3 is very similar to the words in Exodus 15, Deuteronomy 32 and 33, Judges 5 and 2 Samuel 22. Habakkuk 3 contains many liturgical and musical markers, more like a spiritual song in the Psalter than a poem.[3] This chapter expresses trust in deliverance still to come.

At the end of the chapter there is a message of hope to people in great distress.[4] Habakkuk recounts God's faithfulness in Judah's past and reminds them that they can trust God. Psychologists Kathleen Arnold, Kathleen McDermott and Karl Szpunar suggest in their studies that people's ability to envision the future is strongly influenced by their past. That is, you tend to use memories of past experiences to predict what life will be like in the future.[5] Habakkuk used his experience of the past to help shape his belief in the future. They could trust God as He had journeyed with them in the past.

There is a story told of the former President of the United States of America, Benjamin Franklin, who was not a Christian but had great respect for the Bible.[6] He was appointed the American Plenipotentiary to France in 1782 and was often teased by the French intellectuals for his admiration of the Bible. He once used Habakkuk 3:17–19 to amaze a group of these people who despised him. One evening he told them he had a manuscript that contained an amazing ancient poem. When he read Habakkuk 3:17–19, his listeners all responded by saying, 'What a magnificent poem!' He told them where he had read it from and they were amazed.

### Lament

The book of Habakkuk comprises laments, prophetic and woe oracles, and prayer. The different forms of language appear to be used in a purposeful way although the author R.P. Carroll says of Habakkuk, 'a ragbag of traditional elements held together by vision and prayer Habakkuk illustrates the way prophetic books have been put together in an apparently slap-dash fashion'.[7] You may think that as you first read it, but it then appears to take on a more coherent structure as you keep reading it. Over half of the book is written in the language of prayer, so it is unique among the prophetic books. The book of Habakkuk opens with a cry to God using words in the same way that Nahum did. Nahum, however, had a prophecy for Nineveh; this was closer to home. Habakkuk then utters his complaint on the behalf of his people. This is like the words of the psalms, like communal lament. His words are, 'How long, Yahweh?' which are echoed in the Psalms. Psalm 13, 35 and 79 are a few examples.

Psalm 13:1,2 says:

> How long, LORD? Will you forget me for ever?
> How long will you hide your face from me?
> How long must I wrestle with my thoughts
> and day after day have sorrow in my heart?
> How long will my enemy triumph over me?

Psalm 79:1–7 says:

> O God, the nations have invaded your inheritance;
> they have defiled your holy temple,
> they have reduced Jerusalem to rubble.
> They have left the dead bodies of your servants
> as food for the birds of the sky,
> the flesh of your own people for the animals of the wild.
> They have poured out blood like water

all around Jerusalem,
and there is no one to bury the dead.
We are objects of contempt to our neighbours,
of scorn and derision to those around us.
How long, LORD? Will you be angry for ever?
How long will your jealousy burn like fire?
Pour out your wrath on the nations
that do not acknowledge you,
on the kingdoms
that do not call on your name;
for they have devoured Jacob
and devastated his homeland.

Following the prophet's complaint about the evil in his land, Yahweh speaks through Habakkuk, letting the people know that the wrongdoing is to be punished through the Chaldean attack. That must have been challenging for Habakkuk, learning that Yahweh would use the Chaldeans as his agents of change. This can also be called the Arminian doctrine of concurrence. Concurrence happens when two or more events or circumstances are happening or existing at the same time. Judah's enemies were used by God to also judge His people. This is a strange concept, as we ask ourselves, is it possible for God to turn evil into good? How can God use men's evil actions and cause something good to happen? An example of this is in the life of Joseph. It is the idea that divine sovereignty and our own freedom co-exist together in a remarkable tension.[8]

Most of us have been praying for situations in our communities, in our world, where evil seems to flourish. Just this week I was praying for Leah. Leah was one of 110 girls abducted from their school in Dapchi, Nigeria by Islamic State West Africa Province (ISWAP) in February 2018. In March 2018 most of the girls were put into vehicles to go home, but Leah was not among them. She was not released because she refused to convert in exchange for her freedom.[9] The charity Church World Service (CWS) has been campaigning on her behalf. It is a terrible situation, one of many across our world. It is heartbreaking for Leah and her family that two years later we are still waiting for Leah to be released. God does not always answer us straightaway or give us the answers we want or expect. We can trust Him for the big and little situations in our world.

Habakkuk certainly uses the language of lament, the passionate expression of grief. It is born of mourning or sadness about what will happen to Judah. Some think we have lost this ability to lament in church life.[10] There are, however, many examples of lament throughout Scripture. Consider the book of Lamentations, probably written about Jeremiah where he pleads with God over the evil and suffering of the world. Read the Psalms; they include so many songs of lament. And listen to Jesus in Mark 14:36, when he cried out to God, '*Abba*, Father . . . everything is possible for you. Take this cup from me. Yet not what I will, but what you will.'

How do we respond to events that are tragic and moving and have happened in our communities, our countries, over the past few days, weeks and months? Recently, in Northern Ireland, the law was changed to allow abortion up to term for babies with even minor abnormalities, such as club foot or cleft palate. Listen to this: 'A voice is heard in Ramah [and in Newtownards, Belfast and Northern Ireland], mourning and great weeping, Rachel weeping for her children and refusing to be comforted, because they are no more' (Jer. 31:15). Our Christian tradition of the prayer of lament gives us a way of speaking to God during times of deep and incomprehensible loss.

Some of us do not like lament, as it makes us feel uncomfortable. Some even feel it is disrespectful – all those tears and snot. In his book *A Praying Life*, the author Paul Miller says, 'We think laments are disrespectful. God says the opposite. Lamenting shows you are engaged with God in a vibrant, living faith. We live in a deeply broken world. If the pieces of our world are not breaking your heart and you aren't in God's face about them, then . . . you've thrown in the towel.'[11]

Lament may not be a common word in our spiritual lives, but it is woven throughout Scripture. A prayer of lament is a passionate expression of our pain. It is honest and transparent talk with God – telling Him how we are and what we feel. There is no pretence. I think when I have heard people lament then it has often been like a plea for help during a time of distress, or a crying out about injustice. It has the same Hebrew root word as 'to mourn' and 'to wail'.

In several cultures, such as Africa, the Americas and even some Celtic nations, people cry out a mourning lament called the 'death wail' at funerals. Lament can be loud and harsh and extreme, or quiet and broken. This lament is not a structured prayer; it's not about being polite or holding it all together. Lament is an honest expression of pain: 'Lord, I am scared, Lord, I am frightened, I am gutted . . . I don't know what to do . . .' I have prayed these prayers over situations in our world, events in my friends' lives, or even when people have hurt or said all manner of things against my family. I have lamented for the church and for the people around me.

We are facing a difficult situation now and all I can do is lament. Even writing these few words my heart feels like it is splitting in two and I can only turn to God, who sees my heart. Sometimes the words escape as whispers, as quiet as the noises generated from my own beating heart; the sounds made by the turbulence as my heart valves shut between each chamber allowing blood to flow to where it needs to go. In medicine these are represented as the words Lub, Dub.[12] God can hear my heart . . . Lub-DUB . . . lub-DUB . . . lub-DUB.[13] God can hear the sounds my heart makes – there are times I cannot utter the right words, but He hears my heart.

**Let's pray**

Oh Lord,
We confess that often we live our lives according to our agenda.
We can be selfish and self-centred. We do not always put You or others first.
We forget that we are made in Your divine image and should see that in each other.
We do not treat each other and the communities of faith we are a part of with humility and regard.
Instead we attack each other, at times firing arrows.
These are words that hurt, inflict injury and
that make a sham of our own faith.
We know that Your heart must break
when brothers and sisters fall out
or communities divide.

We pray for communities of faith that are struggling with internal strife
and external distractions.
We don't need to know what is happening.

Heal their wounds.
We pray for the shocked and shaken.

The families, homes and communities that need You.
O God, speak to us.
O God, hear our prayer.
We are sorry. We repent. Help us to love.
Help us to hope in that coming day
when You will return.
Amen.

# 8
## Joel

# A Plea for Repentance

I must confess, I approached the book of Joel with a little trepidation. Like many people, I am sure, the book of Joel leaves me confused and even scared at the images of plagues, fire and the end of the world.

When I started writing this book, the idea of a worldwide pandemic was on the distant horizon. Since then, people have talked about the fact that we are living in Old Testament times as we have battled with a worldwide crisis. As of September 2020 there are more than 881,831 deaths worldwide related to the disease Covid-19 caused by the severe acute respiratory syndrome coronavirus 2 (SARS-CoV-2).[1] In the United Kingdom it looks like we are heading out of the first peak of the disease. This is not the case across the world. Countries across Africa and Asia are fighting this virus with populations often in crowded conditions, with acute health issues and a poorly resourced health service. The international rescue committee calls this a 'double emergency of Covid-19' with the grave shortages of ventilators and Intensive Care beds. For some people, especially those working in the front-line services, it feels like the end of the world.

How do we cope when such vivid imagery swamps our minds? What can we learn about prayer?

Joel is another one of the books of the minor prophets that is full of colourful imagery. We know little about Joel himself, but he clearly heard from God. The people of God were living through a great catastrophe as a swarm of locusts had destroyed their crops and land. Joel warns the people of more plagues to come. The book focuses its prophetic judgment on the southern kingdom of Judah.

Sometimes the imagery of the minor prophet books appears alien to us. Very few of us have experienced what the people of Israel went through. Locusts have, however, formed plagues since biblical times. The ancient Egyptians carved images of them on their tombs. Swarms have caused huge devastation to a variety of crops and agriculture. They have been a contributory cause of famines and mass human migrations. In the spring of 1747, a plague of locusts arrived outside Damascus and destroyed most of their crops and vegetation. Ahmad al-Budayri, a local barber, said the locusts 'came like a black cloud. They covered everything: the trees and the crops. May God Almighty save us!'.[2] In 1869 a desert locust plague even reached England, probably from West Africa. At the start of 2020 there has been a plague of locusts that has devastated east Africa. In early 2020 they reached the borders of China where the people are coping with an epidemic of Covid-19. Usual locust activity should decline in late autumn but can continue to June.

## The main character

We do not know a lot about Joel. His name combines the Jewish covenant name of God (Yahweh) with El (God), and literally means 'the one to whom Yahweh is God,' or 'a worshipper of Yahweh'.

All we really know about Joel is what we are told in his book. We also know that there are several people called Joel in the Bible and that his name is nearly as common as John! There was Joel, a chief of the tribe of Simeon,[3] Joel, a chief of the tribe of Gad[4]; one Joel was the brother of Nathan and one of David's mighty men[5] and another Joel was from the Kohath branch of the tribe of Levi who lived during the reign of King Hezekiah of Judah.[6]

The Joel we want to focus on is Joel, son of Pethuel. In Joel 1:1 we are told that: 'The word of the LORD that came to Joel son of Pethuel.' So, we don't know much about Joel apart from the fact that he preached to the people of Judah. He was interested in what was happening in Jerusalem. We can also presume that he was well-educated. His book shows us he was a gifted poet. In Joel 1:13,14 and 2:14,17 Joel speaks about worship in the Temple, so we can presume he was familiar with the Temple and its layout.

### The background

The order of Joel in the traditional Christian Bible and the Jewish text differ. The Masoretic Text is the authoritative Hebrew and Aramaic text of the Jewish *Tanakh*. It was copied, edited and distributed by the Masoretic Jews between the seventh and tenth centuries. It places Joel between Hosea and Amos. The Greek version of the Old Testament, known as the Septuagint, has a different order– Hosea, Amos, Micah, Joel, Obadiah and Jonah. Fragments of Joel chapters 1 and 2 were found in the Dead Sea Scrolls that were discovered in 1949.

There is also some debate as to when the book was written. This is because, unlike most of the other prophetic writers, Joel gave no explicit indication of his time period. Generally, the king of the time is mentioned. An example is the prophet Zephaniah. In Zephaniah 1:1 we are told:

> The word of the LORD that came to Zephaniah son of Cushi, the son of Gedaliah, the son of Amariah, the son of Hezekiah, during the reign of Josiah son of Amon king of Judah . . .

There is a school of thought that suggests that Joel was written after the death of Queen Athaliah of Judah in 835BC. Her grandson Joash succeeded her but was too young to rule, so the priest Jehoiada ruled in his place. If Joel had been around in this time frame, he would not have mentioned the reigning king as there was none. These puzzles of history can be so exciting!

The French theologian and reformer, John Calvin suggests that Joel prophesied earlier than 835BC. He suggests that it was during the time of Jehoram, king of Israel in around 849–842BC.[7] This is because Joel mentions a famine which has been highlighted in historical documents recording that timeframe. However, he also suggests that Joel could have been around during the time of King Manasseh. Certainly, there is some confusion as to when he lived and died. Joel does mention Judah's suffering and some even suggest that Joel 1:14 refers to the destruction of the Temple, so he was around prior to the fall of Jerusalem and the destruction of the Temple.[8] Personally, I do not think this verse makes that clear:

> Declare a holy fast;
> call a sacred assembly.
> Summon the elders
> and all who live in the land
> to the house of the LORD your God,
> and cry out to the LORD.

There is also some debate about whether the events mentioned in Joel are allegorical or literal. While the book describes a terrible plague of locusts, some Jewish theologians suggest that the locusts are an allegorical interpretation of Israel's enemies. Joel tells us that just as the locusts devoured the land, so will the land be destroyed by Judah's enemies unless the nation repents of its sins. Many of the Church Fathers believed that the plague of locusts did not happen. Matthew Henry suggests that the four different types of insects or locusts represent the leaders of armies that attacked Judah over a period of four years.[9] Calvin believed that the locust plague was a literal event. There has also been debate throughout the years about the structure of the book as different versions have different numbers of chapters. The extra chapter is gained by subdividing Joel 2.

There are five translations which have four chapters. These are the:

- Jewish Publication Society's version of the Hebrew Bible (1917)
- Jerusalem Bible (1966)
- New American Bible (Revised Edition, 1970)
- Complete Jewish Bible (1998)
- Tree of Life Version (2015)

Our original King James Bible of 1611 only has three chapters in the book of Joel.

### The main message

Joel is an extraordinary book full of vivid imagery and poetry. He certainly drew upon his surroundings, reminding us to look at nature: the sun and the moon, the grass and the locusts.

The book may be broken down into the following sections in the NIV:

- There is lament over the plague of locusts and the severe drought (Joel 1:1 – 2:17).
- We are shown how these events have affected agriculture, farmers and the supply of agricultural offerings for the Temple (Joel 1:1–20).
- There is a comparison of the locusts to an army bringing God's judgment (Joel 2:1–11).
- There is a national call to repentance and lament because of God's judgment (Joel 2:12–17).
- There is a promise of future blessings (Joel 2:18 – 3:2).
- There is a promise of future prophetic gifts to all God's people (Joel 2:28–32).
- We are reminded of the coming judgment on the kingdom of Judah's enemies: the Philistines, the kingdoms of Egypt and Edom; also the end of the age (Joel 3:1–21).

As you can see, the book of Joel is an important book, as it has some hard-hitting themes. It is also the first to develop the biblical idea of the 'day of the LORD' (2:1), dependent on when you think it was written. While Obadiah may have mentioned this terrifying event first in Obadiah 15, Joel gives us more specific details. He talks about the 'day of the LORD' being days cloaked in darkness, of armies that conquer their enemies like a consuming fire, and even describes the moon turning to blood.

It is suggested that the book covers three main themes:

- The judgment of God's people
- The judgment of their neighbouring nations
- The restoration of God's people through their suffering.[10]

I would suggest that the main themes are as follows:

- In chapter 1 the focus is on the judgment of God. Joel compares the resulting judgment to a plague of locusts.
- In chapters 2 to 3 God calls His people to repent, or they, too, will all be judged.

**About prayer**

Joel is a book that reminds us that God wants His people to turn to Him in prayer. We are reminded that during dark days we can turn to a God of light. In Joel 2 we are reminded that, although we should pray individually, we are also called to corporate prayer. Corporate prayer pattern has been used throughout the history of the church.

Jonathan Graf, the president of the Church Prayer Leaders Network and author of *Restored Power: Becoming a Praying Church One Tweak at a Time*[11] suggests that there are five biblical principles of powerful corporate prayer which are: be desperate, have one focus, speak with one voice, allow God's presence to be at the centre of what we do and be in agreement.

His principle of desperation is illustrated in the book of Ezra. The writer records a time of corporate prayer, as part of a three-day fast, when Ezra was leading a group of Jews back to Jerusalem and they had a dangerous journey ahead of them. Ezra 8:21–23 tells us:

> There, by the Ahava Canal, I proclaimed a fast, so that we might humble ourselves before our God and ask him for a safe journey for us and our children, with all our possessions. I was ashamed to ask the king for soldiers and horsemen to protect us from enemies

on the road, because we had told the king, 'The gracious hand of our God is on everyone who looks to him, but his great anger is against all who forsake him.' So we fasted and petitioned our God about this, and he answered our prayer.

Powerful prayer is often considered to be focused prayer. It can be tough to be focused when you are in a crisis, but we do need to speak with one voice, pleading for God's presence. Using the imagery of 2 Chronicles 6–7 at the dedication of Solomon's Temple, we are reminded that Solomon invited God to come and dwell in the Temple. We know that, because of what Jesus has done for us, God's Spirit lives in us. The Holy of Holies is within us. We don't need to ask for God to dwell with us if we follow Him, but we do need to allow God to manifest His presence. We need to focus on God and to be reminded that He is at the centre of our lives as we praise and worship Him.

In America there is a National Day of Prayer. In fact, it is an annual day of prayer held on the first Thursday of May. People are asked to turn to God and pray for their nation. The President is even required by their law to sign an annual proclamation, encouraging all Americans to pray on this particular day. In early 2020, churches across the UK had a day of prayer, praying together for the government and those working to contain the coronavirus, such as health care personnel, as well as those who are most vulnerable.

When Winston Churchill became prime minister in 1940, one of the first things he did was call a National Day of Prayer prior to the miracle of the evacuation of the British army at Dunkirk. There were a further two national days of prayer in 1943 and 1944 when people stopped work to pray together. The last National Day of Prayer was on 6 July 1947. Corporate prayer is not a new thing. Certainly, throughout the history of the United Kingdom there have been hundreds of national days of prayer. We may not have a national prayer-time but we can participate in corporate prayer in church buildings or via the internet as we battle Covid-19.

Corporate prayer should be an important part of the life of our church. It sits alongside fellowship, biblical teaching, communion and praise. It edifies and unites us as we pray together.

In Joel, the people have cried and lamented as they watched their crops destroyed by locusts. Now they are told to shed tears of repentance before God. In Joel 2:12,13 God calls his people to repent in a corporate act of prayer:

> 'Even now,' declares the LORD,
>     'return to me with all your heart,
>     with fasting and weeping and mourning.'
> Rend your heart
>     and not your garments.
> Return to the LORD your God,
>     for he is gracious and compassionate,
>     slow to anger and abounding in love,
>     and he relents from sending calamity.

I think intertwined with the imagery and words of repentance are also the call to lament. The book has very similar linguistic parallels to the language of Amos, Micah, Zephaniah, Jeremiah and Ezekiel. These phrases may have been the liturgical phrases of the day.

In Joel 1:13 we read:

> Put on sackcloth, you priests, and mourn;
>     wail, you who minister before the altar.
> Come, spend the night in sackcloth,

you who minister before my God;
for the grain offerings and drink offerings
are withheld from the house of your God.

We are told in Joel 1:1–17 that the 'day of the LORD', the day
of judgment, is near. The people are to mourn and lament
what has happened. The locusts have destroyed the land, eating everything in their sight. There is not even any grain for a
grain offering to God. If the people lamented, then God would
answer. This is a summons to repent. It differs from other calls to
repent, as we are reminded in Joel 2:13,14 that God is 'gracious
and compassionate'. He is also 'slow to anger and abounding
in love'. (Zephaniah called the people to repent as judgment
was coming.[12] Isaiah called the people to repent while God is
near.[13] Jeremiah's call to repent is before judgment.[14])

We know God did answer and they returned to Jerusalem.
The Exile ended, some of the foreign nations were subdued
and the Temple was rebuilt. The call for repentance is also for
today. God will judge His people on the day of judgment,
unless they repent and turn to Him. Peter quoted from Joel
in Acts 2:16–21, when he addressed the crowd on the day of
Pentecost. He said:

. . . this is what was spoken by the prophet Joel:
'In the last days, God says,
I will pour out my Spirit on all people.
Your sons and daughters will prophesy,
your young men will see visions,
your old men will dream dreams.
Even on my servants, both men and women,
I will pour out my Spirit in those days,
and they will prophesy.

I will show wonders in the heavens above
and signs on the earth below,
blood and fire and billows of smoke.
The sun will be turned to darkness
and the moon to blood
before the coming of the great and glorious day of the Lord.
And everyone who calls
on the name of the Lord will be saved.'

Several years ago, as I mentioned earlier, we went to Jerusalem for my husband's fortieth birthday. I booked the flights and accommodation and we went on our own – no planned tour. We had never been before. It was an extraordinary trip – so emotional. One day we went to the site of the Pool of Siloam, which was cut out of the rock on the southern slope of the City of David. It was originally located outside the walls of the Old City and was fed by the waters of the Gihon Spring. In the Gospel of John, Jesus sent a man who was 'blind from birth' to the same pool to be healed (John 9:7). The pool was rediscovered during excavation work for a sewer in 2004. During our visit I sat on a bench outside to rest. There was a Jewish man sitting on the other end of the bench. He started coughing. As a respiratory nurse specialist, I listened to him, wondered if he had chronic obstructive pulmonary disease (COPD) and offered him my unopened water bottle. He got up, started shouting at me in Hebrew and left me wondering why he was so angry. As I sat there, I remembered Jesus words recorded in John 7:37,38:

Let anyone who is thirsty come to me and drink. Whoever believes in me, as Scripture has said, rivers of living water will flow from within them.

God will not turn people away if they ask Him for a drink. They do, however, have to turn to him. I could not force that man to take a drink – I could only offer it. The book of Joel reminds me that judgment is coming but that God is also 'gracious and compassionate'. As a book it prompts us to pray – it is one that makes us fall on our knees and plead and lament with God for the people that do not know Him. This may be dramatic, but we are living in uncertain times. The desert locust has threatened Africa, the Middle East and Asia for centuries. When I started writing this book at the beginning of 2020, the locusts had shredded the countryside, sweeping through east Africa, eating twice their bodyweight in food. Ethiopia, Kenya and Somalia are all struggling with unprecedented swarms of these insects and they are now heading to China. People will die from lack of food.

Since the first cases of the acute respiratory syndrome in the Wuhan municipality of China, probably originating from a wet market in December 2019, cases have shot up in numbers. The Novel coronavirus spread, infecting thousands of people in Asia, Australia, America, Europe, Africa and North America. On the 11 March 2020 Covid-19 was declared a pandemic by the World Health Organization. There have even been predictions that the virus could infect between 60 and 70 per cent of the planet, worse than the 1918 Spanish Flu pandemic.[15] It is estimated that the death rate in two-thirds of the world will be 1–2 per cent. In some countries this could be as high as 4 per cent. It is difficult to know when this pandemic will end.

Our world is changing at a dramatic rate with news of fires, volcanoes and disease. These events, as in the time of Joel, should send us back to God, pleading for our world. He is 'gracious and compassionate'. He will listen if we ask.

**Let's pray**

> God of mercy,
> We pray for those affected by the current viruses that are
>     present in our communities, whether that be Covid-19
>     or influenzae. Comfort those whose loved ones are seri-
>     ously ill or who have died from it. Bring peace to those
>     living with uncertainty. Stabilise economies, strengthen
>     health care systems and be strength for those who need
>     it. We pray particularly for health care workers, leaders,
>     those in public service or those who have the potential
>     to be at risk from catching the disease.
> Strengthen those who are risking their own lives to care for
>     people.
>
> God of mercy,
> Turn Your face to hear those who call out to You – those
>     people who have seen what is happening in the world
>     around them and know that they need You.
>
> God of mercy,
> We pray that You will remember Your people – those who
>     do not know that You have sent Your Son to die for them.
>     Those who are still waiting for their Messiah to come.
>
> God of mercy,
> Hear our prayers.
>
> We know that You are 'gracious and compassionate'.
> We know that You offer us salvation through your Son.
> Amen.

# 9
## Obadiah

# Remember Who God Is

Obadiah is one of those books that appears to move every time you open your Bible. My husband always tells people to use the index if they can't find it! You will find it nestled between Amos and Jonah. In Judaism, Obadiah is one of the twelve prophets in the final section of the Nevi'im, which is the second main division of the Hebrew Bible (the *Tanakh*). It sits between the Torah (instruction) and *Ketuvim* (writings). In Christianity, Obadiah is considered one of the minor prophets.

At first glance it appears an obscure book, the shortest in the Old Testament, and consists of only twenty-one verses. It does, however, have a lot to say. Remember what I said before about small packages? *The Infographic Bible* by Karen Sawrey informs us that God has spoken through creation 1,015 direct promises, 769 messages through his prophets, 141 writings, 86 pictures, 54 messages from angels, 64 reports about Him, a burning bush and a donkey![1] He certainly used Obadiah to remind us that there will be divine judgment against those who persecute God's people. This is a promise that Jesus reminds us of in Matthew 24 and what we see in Revelation 19.

**The main character**

Interestingly, according to the *Talmud*, Obadiah is said to have been a convert to Judaism rather than a native of Judah. He is thought to have come from Edom, and was a descendant of Eliphaz, who was one of Job's friends. The *Talmud* is the comprehensive written version of the Jewish oral law (*Mishnah*), its rabbinic discussions and commentaries (*Gemara*). Obadiah was the servant of Ahab and was himself an Edomite. Obadiah received the gift of prophecy for having hidden 100 prophets from the persecution of Jezebel, the wife of King Ahab.[2] We also know that Obadiah means 'servant of the Lord' or 'worshipper of Yahweh', so we can presume he did convert to Judaism.

As with many of the minor prophets, it is difficult to be confident about the date of the book. This is partly since we do not know much about Obadiah or his family. The date is therefore determined based on the prophecy outlined in the book. We know that Edom is to be destroyed because of its pride and lack of belief in God. They also did not defend Israel, to whom they were related, when Israel was attacked.

What is confusing is that there are two major historical events in which the Edomites could have done this. The first is during 853–841 BC when Jerusalem was invaded by Philistines and Arabs. This was during the reign of King Jehoram and the time of the prophet Elijah. The other event was in 607–586 BC when Jerusalem was attacked by King Nebuchadnezzar II of Babylon.[3] This resulted in the Babylonian exile of Israel.[4] This would have made Obadiah a contemporary of the prophet Jeremiah. Most scholars agree that Obadiah would have been around in the sixth century.[5] Obadiah was probably referring to the destruction of Jerusalem by King Nebuchadnezzar II.

It is also suggested that the writings of Jeremiah are so like Obadiah that they had the same source.[6] This may seem odd as we have accepted it as part of the canon of Scripture. Prophetic writings were, however, considered something that could be copied and circulated.[7]

W.P. Brown suggests that the best argument places Obadiah in the 840s BC, making him earlier than the prophet Joel.[8] The basis of this argument is that Edom could not have overcome Jerusalem by themselves and would have had to be allies of the Philistines and the Arabs. I personally think this is a weak argument because by 607BC Judah had been through a lot and they had poor defences against any invading enemy.

There are also twelve men named Obadiah who appear in Scripture. We cannot say with certainty which Obadiah our Obadiah was.[9] Certainly, some writers believe he was the third captain sent out by Ahaziah against Elijah although, again, that would place him earlier than 607–586BC. What we do know is that the nine minor prophets mentioned in the books of Obadiah through to Malachi lived during a terrible time in Israelite history, a time which lasted 200 years.[10]

## The background

This was a particularly difficult time for the people of Israel, as their lives were disrupted by constant wars and rumours. It was bookended by the Assyrian threat in the eighth century, the Babylonia exile in the sixth, as well as the hopeful age of restoration in the late sixth and early fifth centuries. The identity of our Obadiah is shrouded in mystery, but his message is clear to the Edomites– there would be a day of reckoning.

### The Edomites

Edom was one of the ancient kingdoms in Transjordan and was situated between Moab in the north-east, Arabah to the west and the Arabian Desert to the south and east. It is now amalgamated between Israel and Jordan. They were thought to have descended from Esau, Jacob's older twin brother. Jacob deceived his father, with some help from his mother, and stole Esau's birthright. The story is told in Genesis 25:21–34 and Genesis 27. The Edomite people first established their kingdom (Edom) in the southern area of modern-day Jordan. They are mentioned in Numbers 20 when they refused to let the Israelites pass through their lands on the way to the Promised Land. Numbers 20:14–21 says:

> Moses sent messengers from Kadesh to the king of Edom, saying:
> 'This is what your brother Israel says: you know about all the hardships that have come on us. Our ancestors went down into Egypt, and we lived there many years. The Egyptians ill-treated us and our ancestors, but when we cried out to the LORD, he heard our cry and sent an angel and brought us out of Egypt.
> 'Now we are here at Kadesh, a town on the edge of your territory. Please let us pass through your country. We will not go through any field or vineyard, or drink water from any well. We will travel along the King's Highway and not turn to the right or to the left until we have passed through your territory.'
>
> But Edom answered:
> 'You may not pass through here; if you try, we will march out and attack you with the sword.'

The Israelites replied:

'We will go along the main road, and if we or our livestock drink any of your water, we will pay for it. We only want to pass through on foot – nothing else.'

Again they answered:

'You may not pass through.'

Then Edom came out against them with a large and powerful army. Since Edom refused to let them go through their territory, Israel turned away from them.

Later they moved to Judah and the area of the Negev down to Timna prior to the destruction of Judah by King Nebuchadnezzar II in 587/86BC. They took advantage of the already-weakened state of Judah.[11]

The Edomite people were considered a proud people. God speaks through Obadiah and calls them that in Obadiah 3:

> The pride of your heart has deceived you,
> you who live in the clefts of the rocks
> and make your home on the heights,
> you who say to yourself,
> 'Who can bring me down to the ground?'

I must confess I do wonder how much of Edom's hatred is the consequence of Esau's lost inheritance. Yes, the Edomites were descended from Jacob's brother Esau but they hated Israel, refused to help Israel in their need, sold them as slaves, and were abusive to them while they were exiled to Babylon. It reminds us that, although God was able to forgive Jacob, there are always consequences to our actions. Through Obadiah, God declares his judgment over Edom. God promises that there will be a day when he will 'destroy the wise men of Edom' because of the 'violence' against Jacob (vv. 8,10).

Obadiah prophesies that Edom will be destroyed (v. 10), erased from history.

Obadiah addresses key questions that the Israelites would have asked God during this time.

- Why was this happening?
- Why do the godless nations of the world triumph?
- Will God remember His covenant with His people?

These are huge questions, but Obadiah is careful with his words; he reminds us of the following big truths:

- God (despite Israel's sin) will judge those who afflict his people (Obadiah 1–15).
- God will keep His promises to his people (Obadiah 16–18).
- Israel will be a blessing to the whole world (Obadiah 19–21).

**The main message**

Not only had Edom failed their brother nation Israel, but they thought themselves greater than they were. They dared to mock, steal from and even harm God's chosen people. In the years prior to this time, the surrounding nations would have been careful how they dealt with God's people. God would not stand idly by and let His people suffer forever.

## Pride

We know that the nation of Edom had been found guilty of pride before the Lord in Obadiah 3. Through Obadiah, God reminded Edom of their poor treatment of His people (vv. 12– 14) and promised redemption, not to the Edomites but to the people of Judah (vv. 17,18). The nation of Edom, which eventually disappeared into history, remains one of the prime examples of the truth found in Proverbs 16:18:

> Pride goes before destruction,
> a haughty spirit before a fall.

We are challenged to not be so self-sufficient that we forget about God. Obadiah offers us a stark reminder that we need to place ourselves under God's authority and His guidance. I think sometimes we forget that pride is a sin.

We are reminded of this in Mark 7:21–23. It can become a barrier, a hurdle between us and God. God hates it when we are proud because a proud person thinks they are more important than someone else.

I have been in church ministry now for more than twenty-five years. There have been times when I have had to check myself about pride, particularly as I have a very charismatic and gifted husband. His work has opened doors for me to meet and greet many wonderful people. I must be careful not to get too proud of the things I have been able to do or the places I have been. Often God reminds me not to be proud. Several years ago, we were invited to 10 Downing Street as Malcolm was involved in an event celebrating the nominations of the Faithworks

Award. I was thrilled and excited to go . . . and a little proud. God reminded me to keep looking at Him. Initially, I was not allowed to attend, as I had been blacklisted. I did not pass the initial security. Mad – right! It all stemmed back to my student days when I used to write and protest about a range of things, from the implementation of the poll tax, which only occurred in Scotland, to the suggestion of cancelling school meals. I really believed my letters were making a difference. They obviously were!

Finally, I could go. I stood in the reception room of number 10 with a friend waiting for the then prime minister Gordon Brown to enter the room. I decided I needed to use the bathroom, so my friend and I headed to the toilets. What I didn't know was that we missed the prime minister arriving. We went back down the stairs, chatting about how disappointed we were, when a door opened, and I went colliding into Gordon Brown. Later we laughed about it so much. I may not have a photo of me shaking the prime minister's hand as I came back from using the bathroom, but I don't need it.

You may have heard the hit song 'It's Hard to be Humble' by Mac Davis. If not, have a listen to it on YouTube!

## About prayer

I found that this book really challenged me about my attitude. I think we can become quite proud of what we have achieved, or what we have. Maybe it is because we are bombarded with messages from all around us to be better, aim higher, gain followers, or become famous. I was really challenged about how I spoke to God. Why is it we can so easily fall into prideful behaviour, and struggle to be humble? The obvious answer is our sin.

Culturally, it is also acceptable if you have followers and an ego to go with it. We celebrate celebrity with all its fame, popularity and prestige and accept the egos and pride that are part of it. We accept that celebrities may even have strange requests prior to a concert or filming. These are often included in a tour rider, which is a document that includes the rules and criteria for a performer. According to the celebrity journalist Liat Kornowski in the HuffPost US, the singer Mariah Carey has been known to ask for buckets of spicy fried chicken wings.[12] The singer Lady Gaga has been said to request white leather couches, fresh roses and black satin drapes and old rock posters of David Bowie, Queen, Elton John and Billie Holiday.[13] Some riders I can understand, but some are just because they can!

We can get caught up in celebrity status and what it means in our culture. We then expect our leaders to be the same. The axiom that leadership is all about influence can be misinterpreted as a faulty belief about leaders. We are led to believe that a true leader always gets their way. We have this idea that a great leader stands out above everyone else. Isn't this sounding like the story of King Nebuchadnezzar and his golden statue, in Daniel 3:1? The issue is that our pride can become an idol, a huge golden statue. This pressure to stand out fuels our already fractured human egos that are all too ready to become haughty and proud. We can deceive ourselves, thinking more highly of ourselves than is true. That can lead to a real battle between our ego and our humility. What we may consider as a normal ego can become infected by narcissistic attitudes and tendencies. We can even focus so much on our own personal power that we forget who and why we serve in the first place.

We can all think of images of proud people asking God to keep them humble, but this is something we need to do. I do not think it is a prayer that I pray enough. Truthfully, I think I'm scared to pray this prayer, but I should not worry as God has used so many crazy circumstances, such as the story above, to keep my eyes on Him. I also think that I have been so blessed to have some fantastic examples of Christians in my life who, despite being well known and famous in the world's eyes, are never too busy to hold a door open for someone, to meet a need even if they don't have to, or clean the church toilets during the week. One wonderful lady I know is quite happy to clean toilets even though she has the prestige or the money to pay someone else. These people have exhibited true servant-hearted leadership, not allowing pride to cloud their vision of what is around them.

Obadiah reminds us to not let pride in our own abilities block our vision. I am not saying 'don't celebrate'. I am saying 'remember who we should give thanks to'. Reading and studying the book of Obadiah, I am reminded that I can only see that path in front of me if my eyes are turned to God. I need His help, His strength, His wisdom, not my own, to live this life. I am so dependent on Him. All I have, He has given me.

The joy of knowing Him should be more than the joy of titles, your name in lights, or initials after your name. In this book we are reminded, again and again through the twenty-one verses, of the awesomeness of God, that God keeps His promises, that we can trust Him. Doesn't that make you want to praise God? Doesn't that make you look beyond yourself and what you have achieved? The lessons of Obadiah are timeless. Don't let pride get in the way. God is watching how we treat other people. God shall judge the wicked and reward those who do good.[14]

**Let's pray**

Father,
Sometimes we are so proud and don't think we need You.
It's as if we just pop in for a chat.
Please remind us of who You are.
We know the whole earth is Yours.
Help us to breathe in and out.
To remember that our very breath is from You.
In Jesus' name.
Amen.

# 10
## Zechariah

# A Call for Hope in a Hopeless Time

The year 2020 is the seventy-fifth anniversary of Victory in
Europe Day (VE Day). It is the day on which we celebrate the
formal acceptance by the Allies of the Second World War of
Nazi Germany's unconditional surrender of its armed forces
on 8 May 1945. This anniversary is especially poignant as it's
unlikely that at the next big anniversary there will be anyone
around who can talk about it.

I love listening to all the documentaries of people who lived
through the First World War. It reminds me of the stories my
granny used to share about what life was like before and after
the war years.

Zechariah is thought to have lived and worked after the devastation of Jerusalem. His book has so many messages to share
with us. There is so much that we can learn from it that I have
summarised his main points.

This book is ultimately a call for hope to the people of Judah
in what appeared to be a hopeless time. Zechariah was a man of
dreams who reminds us of the importance of trusting God. He
had eight dreams in total, which are contained in the fourteen
chapters of the book. These dreams are full of vivid imagery
and symbolism. They start with a picture of where they are and

end with the restoration of Jerusalem. His dreams spoke to the people of his time but also contain prophecies of the coming Messiah. This hope refreshed the exiles returning to Jerusalem.

Zechariah was probably born in Babylon. Ezekiel and Jeremiah wrote before the fall of Jerusalem although it is thought they continued to prophesy in the early years post-exile. Zechariah followed them and was a contemporary of the prophet Haggai, living in a post-exilic world after the fall of Jerusalem in 587/6BC. Many scholars have suggested that Zechariah was influenced by Ezekiel's visions and drama.[1] We can date his writings to 520–518BC as Zechariah mentions being under the rule of Darius the Great, at the time of Haggai. Haggai dealt with the present and the immediate problems facing the people of Judah; Zechariah mentions now but looks to the distant future.

### The main character

There are approximately thirty men named Zechariah in the Old Testament. His name means 'Yahweh has remembered', which sums up Zechariah's message. We know that Zechariah was a priest as well as a prophet and was a contemporary of the prophet Haggai. He mentions Zerubbabel, who was a governor of the Achaemenid Empire's province Yehud Medinata and grandson of Jehoiachin, the penultimate king of Judah. Zerubbabel led the first group of Jews from their Babylonian captivity back to Judah under the reign of Cyrus the Great, the king of the Achaemenid Empire. He then laid the foundation of the Second Temple in Jerusalem soon after. The prophet Haggai identifies Zerubbabel as the governor of Judah after the return from exile. These contemporaries were real heroes, so Zechariah kept good company. Zechariah shared their concern about the importance of having a building dedicated to God at the centre of their community.

Sadly, there are some people who think that Zechariah had a sad death. It is suggested that Zechariah is the priest mentioned by Jesus in Matthew 23:35 who was murdered by the rebellious Jews in the sanctuary:

> And so upon you will come all the righteous blood that has been shed on earth, from the blood of righteous Abel to the blood of Zechariah son of Berekiah, whom you murdered between the temple and the altar.

It is unclear whether he is the same person. We do know, however, that Zechariah tells us in chapter 1:1 that he is the son of Berekiah, son of Iddo. Perhaps he lived a long life and saw the Temple being built. Certainly, Ezra tells us in Ezra 5:1,2:

> Now Haggai the prophet and Zechariah the prophet, a descendant of Iddo, prophesied to the Jews in Judah and Jerusalem in the name of the God of Israel, who was over them. Then Zerubbabel son of Shealtiel and Joshua son of Jozadak set to work to rebuild the house of God in Jerusalem. And the prophets of God were with them, supporting them.

We also know that Jesus called him 'righteous'. What, then, does he teach us, and what was his message? This book is scattered with imagery, poetry and prose. There is so much that we can learn from it that I have summarised his main points as we are only skimming the surface in this chapter.

## The background

Darius the Great was the king of kings of the Achaemenid Empire (the first Persian Empire). He reigned from 522BC until his death in 486BC and is mentioned in the books of Ezra, Nehemiah, Haggai, and Zechariah. He was the king of kings when the Persian Empire was at its peak. Their lands included much of West Asia, parts of the Caucasus, parts of the Balkans lands, most of the Black Sea coastal regions, Central Asia as far as the Indus Valley in the far east and north-east Africa including Egypt, Libya and coastal Sudan.[2]

Darius organised the empire by dividing it into provinces and placing satraps, or provincial governors, to govern them. Yehud Medinata was the Arabic name for the provincial area of old Judah. He inherited the land of Judah after the eighteen-month siege of Jerusalem under King Nebuchadnezzar in 589BC. By then the country's elite were exiled in Babylon, including the priests and royal family. Those in exile were told by the prophets to make their homes there, knowing they would be in exile for a while. Then, in 539BC, Cyrus the Great overtook the Babylonians. In the first year of his reign he produced an edict declaring slaves could go back to their own lands and choose their own religion, which was found carved on the Cyrus Cylinder or Cyrus Charter. This is an ancient clay cylinder which praises King Cyrus as a benefactor of the citizens of Babylonia, for repatriating displaced people and restoring places of religion across Mesopotamia because of his edict. It is written in Akkadian cuneiform script and could be viewed as the first statement on human rights. It was discovered in the ruins of Babylon, or modern-day Iraq, in 1879 and is currently in the British Museum in London. On 14 October 1971,

Princess Ashraf Pahlavi of Iran presented the secretary general of the United Nations with a replica of the cylinder, saying that 'the heritage of Cyrus was the heritage of human understanding, tolerance, courage, compassion and, above all, human liberty'.[3] It is still seen as an artefact of great importance.

A few years ago, Malcolm and I visited room 52 of the British Museum. They run tours of the artefacts of the ancient biblical times in the museum, so we went on one. We ended up standing in front of the famous Cyrus Cylinder and I cried. I think I reflected on what this would have meant to the Israelites of the day. I can't explain how important this must have been to those enslaved in Babylon. It was extraordinary that such an edict was given. Not only were the people released but they were even given back the sacred vessels which had been taken from the First Temple and a considerable sum of money with which to buy building materials.

The book of Ezra tells us that the work recommenced under the exhortations of the prophets, and when the authorities asked the Jews what right they had to build a temple, they were able to refer to the decree of Cyrus. It was a gift that kept on giving! God truly moved Cyrus's heart to let the Jewish people go home. There were no plagues to make him change his mind, no need for a Moses and his staff. A reminder than even when circumstances seem set against us, God can help change the mind of tyrants and kings.

So, the first group of Jewish exiles returned in 538BC, under Sheshbazzar, a prince of Judah, who then became the post-exilic governor of Judah. Sheshbazzar is mentioned in the Bible four times, and there are some who suggest that Sheshbazzar and Zerubbabel were the same person or that Zerubbabel carried on his work. Certainly, after the death of Cyrus in 530BC, King Darius consolidated power and built these manageable districts overseen by governors. Zerubbabel was appointed by Darius as governor over the district of Yehud Medinata.

Zechariah was prophesying at this time, focusing on encouraging those who had returned from exile to the rebuilding of the Temple. The Persian Empire encouraged the rebuilding of the Temple, hoping to keep cordial relationships in Yehud Medinata. They may have thought it was good politics; the Jewish people saw it as a blessing from God.

## The main message

The language of the book is mainly in prose although the oracles or prophecies are in a more poetic style. This is like Jeremiah, Daniel, Haggai and Malachi. The words of God are emphasised using poetry, making it richer and stimulating the imagination. Many of the images are repeated or only mentioned in the second line of the poetry to stand out. The primary theme of the book is to encourage the people of Jerusalem through the eight visions. The book is split into three main sections. These are as follows:

### Chapters 1 to 6

The book begins with an introduction which recalls the nation's history. This is a solemn warning to the people of Jerusalem and Judah. They were told not to be like their ancestors who did evil in God's sight. We read in Zechariah 1:1–6:

> In the eighth month of the second year of Darius, the word of the LORD came to the prophet Zechariah son of Berekiah, the son of Iddo:
>
> 'The LORD was very angry with your ancestors. Therefore tell the people: this is what the LORD Almighty says: "Return to me,"

declares the LORD Almighty, "and I will return to you," says the LORD Almighty. Do not be like your ancestors, to whom the earlier prophets proclaimed: this is what the LORD Almighty says: "Turn from your evil ways and your evil practices." But they would not listen or pay attention to me, declares the LORD. Where are your ancestors now? And the prophets, do they live for ever? But did not my words and my decrees, which I commanded my servants the prophets, overtake your ancestors?

'Then they repented and said, "The LORD Almighty has done to us what our ways and practices deserve, just as he determined to do."'

This is then followed by a series of eight visions, which Zechariah had all in one night. They appear to be eight conversations with God about the stuff of everyday life, but they are packed with encouragements and rich truths. Initially we may think that they are conversations about small areas of our lives that we need to allow God to change. Don't rely on your own strength; remember God is sovereign; remember who should be at the centre of your life. These are not small things. These are gigantic facts that should change us. Allow God to remind you of these things as you pray to Him.

**The first vision** in Zechariah 1:7–11 was of a man mounted on a red horse. 'He was standing among the myrtle trees in a ravine. Behind him were red, brown and white horses.' Zechariah is told by the angel that this is a heavenly patrol guarding the earth. Zechariah asks how long, and he is encouraged as God tells him that He is merciful, and that the Temple will be rebuilt. Read Zechariah verses 1:14–17.

The **second vision** in Zechariah 1:18–21 is of horns and craftsmen. The four horns are the four nations that lead to the breaking up of Israel. God will use the craftsmen to subdue these nations. God wins.

The **third vision** in Zechariah 2:1–5 is of 'a man with a measuring line'. He is measuring Jerusalem – its width and length. In this vision an angel acts as an intermediary between God and the prophet, similar to what we can see when we read the book of Daniel. Certainly, his book accounts for many of the mentions of angels in the Bible. There is no clear reason for this. It could simply be illustrating the battle between good and evil, angels and Satan.

The angel tells the man the following:

> Then I looked up, and there before me was a man with a measuring line in his hand. I asked, 'Where are you going?'
>
> He answered me, 'To measure Jerusalem, to find out how wide and how long it is.'
>
> While the angel who was speaking to me was leaving, another angel came to meet him and said to him: 'Run, tell that young man, "Jerusalem will be a city without walls because of the great number of people and animals in it. And I myself will be a wall of fire around it," declares the LORD , "and I will be its glory within."'

How thrilling, how exciting. What would you say if you received this promise that God would come and be at the centre of your town or city? This is an image of a Temple that will be rebuilt and echoes of a future promise when the Son of Man would come and dwell among us. There is also a reminder of how God wants an intimate relationship with us. God holds us close; we are 'the apple of his eye' (Zech. 2:8). He will protect us because He loves us. At the end of this vision, Zechariah alludes to not only the restoration of Jerusalem but that God is sovereign over all. God may be the God of Judah, but He is also God of the whole earth. Zechariah 2:11 says, 'Many nations will be joined with the LORD in that day and will become my people. I will live among you and you will know that the LORD Almighty has sent me to you.'

The **fourth vision** is in Zechariah 3:1–10. Zechariah has a vision of Joshua, the high priest, and Satan. In this vision, Joshua is put on trial, but God forgives his sins. He replaces his dirty clothes with new ones, so he could do what he was called to do.

The **fifth vision** in Zechariah 4:1–15 tells of the lampstand and the olive trees. The foundation of the new Temple had been built under the leadership of Zerubbabel. He may have been a person of power and position, but his strength came from God. God reminds us that He fulfils his promises (Hag. 2:8,9), even if He used people to do this. He gives them strength.

The **sixth vision** in Zechariah 5:1–5 is about 'a flying scroll'. He looks up and sees a flying scroll, with writing on both sides of it. Zechariah is told that it symbolises a curse that would go out affecting those who are sinful. It is thought to also symbolise the sinful people taken to captivity in Babylon. It can also refer to the fact that God's law should be central in our lives.

The **seventh vision** in Zechariah 5:5–11 is about a woman in a basket. It seems a strange picture, but for Zechariah these were normal everyday things: candlesticks, lampstands and olive trees. The sin in Israel is depicted by a woman in a basket. The sin is contained in the basket and taken away. She is taken away to Shinar which is the site of the Tower of Babel. This is where the people were scattered, as they thought they were more important than God.

The **eighth vision** is in Zechariah 6:1–15. The vision focuses on four chariots. It is as if we started with four horses and end with chariots. It is a reminder that God is in control of the whole earth. The first vision encourages God's people that there will be restoration, the final vision encourages them that God wins – He has won the final battle. Can you imagine how encouraging that would have been to a people living with centuries of ongoing conflict? Since the start of the nineteenth century there has been a war in every decade. These are just a list of the wars across the world from 1990–2000. Imagine these involved your country, your homeland, over 200 years.

- 1990–98        Indonesian military operations in Aceh
- 1990–ongoing   DHKP/C insurgency in Turkey
- 1990–94        Rwandan Civil War
- 1990–95        Tuareg rebellion
- 1990–90        Mindanao crisis
- 1991–91        Operation Traira
- 1991–91        Ten-Day War in Israel
- 1991–92        1991–1992 South Ossetia War
- 1991–94        Djiboutian Civil War
- 1991–95        Croatian War of Independence
- 1991–2002      Sierra Leone Civil War
- 1991–2002      Algerian Civil War

The section on visions ends with one last picture. The people of Judah were to collect their precious metal and make a silver and gold crown. This was to be placed on the head of Joshua, the high priest. It was a symbolic reminder of a future truth, that one day a messiah would come. He would be crowned King of kings. The Temple would also be rebuilt – people in Judah and from far away would help build it. A 'Branch' will also build the Temple of the Lord. God didn't just want to rebuild the

Temple, He wanted to rebuild His people, give them a future and a hope.

> A shoot will come up from the stump of Jesse;
> from his roots a Branch will bear fruit.
>
> *Isa. 11:1*

God didn't just want to rebuild the Temple, He wanted to rebuild His people, give them a future and a hope.

### *Chapters 7 and 8*

Zechariah chapters 7 and 8 are delivered to the people about two years later, in the fourth year of King Darius's reign. These chapters are an encouraging address to the people, assuring them of God's presence and blessing. They are also a reminder to God's people that God wants people who will fast and pray with sincere hearts, not just because it is tradition or ritual to do so. This true and transparent relationship with God will lead to altered actions. Devout faith will be demonstrated not by ritual, but by kindness and mercy. We will show kindness and mercy to those around us. We will care for the widow, the orphan, the poor and the alien in our land. This is a call repeated in the messages of the minor prophets and repeated in the New Testament:

> But Samuel replied:
> 'Does the LORD delight in burnt offerings and sacrifices
> as much as in obeying the LORD?
> To obey is better than sacrifice,
> and to heed is better than the fat of rams.'
>
> *1 Sam. 15:22*

My sacrifice, O God, is a broken spirit;
a broken and contrite heart
you, God, will not despise.

*Ps. 51:17*


For I desire mercy, not sacrifice,
and acknowledgment of God rather than burnt offerings.

*Hos. 6:6*


But go and learn what this means: 'I desire mercy, not sacrifice.'
For I have not come to call the righteous, but sinners.

*Matt. 9:13*


## Chapters 9 to 14

This section consists of two 'oracles' or 'burdens':

- The first oracle is in Zechariah chapters 9–11. It provides an outline of the course of God's dealings with His people Israel to the time of the coming of the Messiah.
- The second oracle is in Zechariah 12 – 14 and helps us to focus on the glories that await Israel in the latter days.

The theologian and writer Colin Sinclair[4] suggests that the book is split into:

Chapters 1–8: The Temple is rebuilt. This is about God's chosen people and the rebuilding of the Temple.

Chapter 9–14: The period after the Temple is rebuilt. This focuses on the future, the new Temple. This is about the promise of the coming of the Messiah and His kingdom.

Chapters 1 to 8 seem easier to understand as Zechariah endorses Haggai's message to those who have returned from exile to rebuild the Temple. Chapters 9 to 14 are a little

confusing. We can understand them better this side of Jesus'
death and resurrection, but it must have been complicated for
the people of sixth-century Judah. It would be like having a
flatpack with no instructions; or a large jigsaw, and being told
to put it together when you don't have the box with a picture
on the lid. These chapters are like the words and imagery of
Daniel 7 – 12 or the book of Revelation. They are described
as symbolic prophecies of the end times.[5] They highlight that
we are living in a wicked world and that God will punish the
wicked. They also encourage us to remain faithful to the end.

In Zechariah 9, he encourages the fearful remnant to trust
God. They are reminded of God's strength in Zechariah 9:9–13.

**About prayer**

It is these verses that encouraged me as a young Christian. I was
14 years old, new to faith and my family did not know who
Jesus really was. I constantly prayed that they would have a
living, active faith. I am ashamed to say that after six months of
praying this prayer I became despondent. I didn't understand
why their eyes weren't opened to God's amazing grace. I had
been reading through the Bible from cover to cover and was
currently reading through Zechariah. I didn't know the history
of Judah, that the nation had been shattered, that more than
20,000 people had been captured, about a quarter of the population, and taken to Babylon for seventy years. I didn't know
that they had begun to give up hope. This chapter, this book,
taught me to persevere in prayer. I was reminded that I was to
talk to God, and He would do the rest.

Zechariah encourages the weak and frightened remnant of
people that they could trust God. They probably felt God had

forgotten them, abandoned them. They needed to be reminded that there was hope in a hopeless situation. The people were reminded to pray – to ask God for His help. Again, and again God says, 'I will' – see Zechariah 9:8; 9:10,11; 9:13.

God's command in Zechariah 10:1 is to 'ask for rain'. They were simply told to ask. The people have gone through a terrible time. Even their leaders have let them down. God reminds them of who He is, of His promises to them and that they can talk to Him. In Zechariah 10 the pronoun 'I' is used thirteen times, reminding us that God is actively engaged with His people. He wants us to talk to Him even if we don't know how to express ourselves. He mentions a third of the people, saying:

> This third I will put into the fire;
> I will refine them like silver
> and test them like gold.
> They will call on my name
> and I will answer them;
> I will say, 'They are my people,'
> and they will say, 'The LORD is our God.'
>
> *Zech. 13:9*

When I first asked Jesus to be in my life, as I mentioned earlier, I attended a church that believed that women were not allowed to pray out loud in prayer meetings. So many of my conversations with God in church were unheard ones in my head. I was therefore thrilled when I attended a church meeting where they encouraged everyone to pray out loud. I felt inadequate, though, as many of the people I heard praying were very eloquent. Some even seemed to pray for hours! God reminded me that He likes to hear my voice. He doesn't care if I don't use long, fancy words, or pray for hours. He simply wants to hear what I have to say.

Sarah[6] had been a nun for several years and was retraining for another profession. I am not sure why she left her orders. I do know that she still wanted to know God on a deeper level than she had known him. She often asked me questions about my personal faith. I encouraged her to pray with me, so we met once a week to talk to God.

On weeks one to two, Sarah was quiet and I prayed out loud. She told me what she had prayed for.

On weeks three to five, Sarah prayed to Mary out loud. Then on week six we were walking down the road and she told me that she had found out something amazing.

'Debbie', she said, 'I have come to realise that I do not need to pray to Mary. I can pray directly to God my Father because of what Jesus has done. God wants an intimate relationship with me'. Sadly, we have lost touch, but I am sure that knowledge has helped her through the ups and downs of life.

The book of Zechariah teaches us that we can trust God. We can hope in hopeless times because he cares for us. It teaches us that we can pray to Him, tell him our deepest thoughts and He will never turn us away.

**Let's pray**

Father,

Thank You that we can approach Your throne with boldness and assurance that You will listen to us.

Thank You for sending Your Son to die for us so that we can have this relationship with You.

We know You care for us, no matter what is going on around us.

We ask that You help us to listen to You, to learn the art of
listening to Your voice even in the storm.

Help us to be faithful, to help us do what You have called
us to do.

Lord, we need Your strength, Your wisdom, Your help.

In Jesus' name.

Amen.

# 11
## Haggai

# A Call for Strength

Haggai is a small book but is packed full of nutritious food. This is one of the books you may need to dip in and out of. Ruminate, chew the cud – reflect and meditate on what it has to say. It is full of great truths that have helped me shape my prayers.

The book of Haggai is a short book of two chapters that contain a series of messages to God's people eighteen years after they returned from exile in Babylon in 538BC. The book contains four messages to the Jewish people of Jerusalem. Haggai is very specific about dates and times. He even dates his prophecies, down to the day. The first message was on 29 August 520BC (Hag. 1:1), the second on 17 October 520BC (Hag. 2:1), and the final two on 18 December 520BC (Hag. 2:10,20). These messages were given to encourage the people of Judah to finish building the Temple. When they doubted they could do it, God reminded them that He was with them.

### The main character

Hardly anything is known about Haggai. It is possible that he was one of the captives taken to Babylon by King

Nebuchadnezzar. Haggai 2:3 seems to indicate that the prophet had seen Jerusalem before the destruction of the Temple and the Exile in 586BC, meaning he was more than 70 years old by the time he delivered his prophecies; an old man looking back on better days for his nation.

Haggai's name means 'my holiday' or 'festival', possibly an indication of when he was born – near one of the traditional Jewish feasts. Again, this hints at a figure who was born in Judah when they still celebrated their Jewish festivals, such as the three pilgrim festivals of Passover (*Pesach*), the Festival of Weeks (*Shavout*), or the Festival of Tabernacles (*Sukkot*). These were huge festivals – a time of celebration and often national holidays as the people would head to the Temple in Jerusalem and participate in festivities and worship.

Remember that trip to Israel that I planned for Malcolm's birthday? What I had not considered was that the holiday would cover the time of the Festival of Tabernacles. This celebrates the Israelites' journey to the Promised Land. During this festival, many Jewish families live in temporary huts (*Sukkot*) that they have made in their gardens. People also make the pilgrimage to Jerusalem although they have not had to do so since the destruction of the Second Temple. On this occasion, our flights were packed with many orthodox Jews on pilgrimage. These festivals are still important in the Jewish calendar.

So by naming Haggai thus, it would be a little like someone calling their child 'Eve' or 'Holly' if they were born at Christmas.

**The background**

The edict issued by King Cyrus of Persia allowed the Jewish exiles to go back to Judah. Nearly 50,000 Jews returned.[1] They took with them silver and gold, as well as other important articles from Solomon's Temple that were looted by Nebuchadnezzar. These were entrusted to the care of Sheshbazzar, possibly Zerubbabel, and were carried to Jerusalem. Sixteen years after the exiles had returned to Judah, Haggai started his prophecies. His main message was in 520BC, when he commanded the Jews to rebuild the Temple.

Rebuilding the Temple was not an easy project. The construction work stopped because of strong opposition from the locals, and the people turned their energies to rebuilding their houses. It was not until King Darius I became king of the Persian Empire that the rebuilding of the Temple resumed. The work of rebuilding the Temple had been suspended for eighteen years. Haggai and Zechariah encouraged the people to rebuild. They reminded them of the second decree of Darius.[2] It was a renewal of Cyrus's decree to rebuild the Temple.

**The main message**

The people of Judah shifted their focus from God their rescuer to their own physical needs and wants. They became so focused on building up their own homes that they forgot about God's house.

After nearly ten years of living in Bournemouth, we felt stirred to move. God had another role for Malcolm. We were devastated about moving but knew we were called on.

It's never easy leaving a church you have been a part of. You feel like you have left a piece of yourself behind. Our challenge was also where to live, as Malcolm had accepted a job at the Evangelical Alliance based in Kensington, London. We had to find a home that he could commute to and from. One of his work colleagues suggested a new estate on the banks of the Thames, called Thamesmead.

On reading about it, we thought it sounded ideal. It was an area of housing situated across the two Boroughs of Greenwich and Bexley; there was a train link to central London at Abbey Wood and plenty of local buses. I didn't drive at the time, and we had four children. So good access to public transport was essential.

When we went house hunting, it was a sunny day. It was amazing being so close to the Thames. We found a house and put an offer on it. Several months later we moved in. The very next day we awoke to find we were covered in mosquito bites, and we had to spend the next eighteen months that we were there plugging in mosquito repellent at night. The children had to be sprayed with insect repellent before they went into the garden. We knew quite quickly that we had relocated to the wrong place!

The other thing we discovered was that Christians left this 1,000-acre estate each Sunday to attend church. The estate had no place of worship at the centre of it. There were schools, a few shops and a play area. There were some lovely walks along the riverbank. There was a community hall. But no church.

So, with another family we started a house church and engaged with our community, doing litter picks or offering hot chocolate and hot cross buns on Easter Sunday to our neighbours. I am glad to say that there is now a wee church at the centre of that estate. I am not saying what we did was the start of it. To be honest, I am not sure. I just know what it feels like when church life is not at the centre of a community. Thankfully the provision of a worship space and community building are considered in newer developments. What would your community look like if you didn't have your church building, or a community centre? The people of Judah had nearly twenty years to get their priorities straight and build their place of worship.

In Haggai 1:4 God says, through the prophet: 'Is it a time for you yourselves to be living in your panelled houses, while this house remains a ruin?'

He wasn't telling them not to build houses or have a home. The wood for the panelling, however, would have to be imported, probably from Lebanon. That would have been expensive. They were more concerned with their interior design than God's house being built. Haggai challenges us – we must consider our priorities. Judah's priorities should have been to rebuild the Temple.

Haggai had the challenge to get the people to resume construction. He tells them to 'Give careful thought to your ways' (Hag. 1:7). His first sermon contained in chapter 1 rebukes the people for having their priorities all wrong. Haggai tells them that, unless they get their priorities right, there will be a drought. As they listened, God encouraged them:

> 'But now be strong, Zerubbabel,' declares the LORD. 'Be strong, Joshua son of Jozadak, the high priest. Be strong, all you people of the land,' declares the LORD, 'and work. For I am with you,' declares the LORD Almighty.
>
> *Hag. 2:4*

The people of Judah were reminded that it was more important that God was with them than not doing His will. The Temple was not to take God's place. It was not the beauty of the Temple that would be its glory, but the presence of God in it.

Haggai uses the phrase 'the LORD of hosts' (in many versions; see for example ESV). The phrase is seen 285 times in the

Bible; ninety-one of those times it is to be found in the books of Haggai, Zechariah and Malachi. These are the prophets who spoke to Judah after the Exile. The language is important. In *The Message* the words used are 'GOD-of-the-Angel-Armies' (see for example Hag. 1:2, MSG). God is speaking to a nation that have just about been destroyed – He is speaking to the remnant that have returned. These words remind them that God is a warrior, a King and a Judge.

The first message was on 29 August 520BC (Hag. 1:1ff). This message was a clear call to rebuild God's house. The people were challenged about the fact that their houses were rebuilt. Some even had panelled walls, but God's house lay in ruins.

Haggai's second message was on 17 October 520BC (Hag. 2:1ff). The people are reminded of how the Temple looked in the past. They are reminded of its former glory, but also that God had promised to be with them. The Temple may be ruined, but He was with them. Zerubbabel, the governor, and Jehozadak, the high priest, are told to be courageous. This is also a powerful message for us today. We are reminded that God keeps His promises; we can therefore trust Him, we can take courage and be brave in the circumstances we are in.

The final two messages were delivered on 18 December 520BC (Hag. 2:10–19; 20–23). Haggai's third message in Haggai 2:10–19 is one of consecration to the priests. He asks the priests about carrying something holy and what happens when it meets something that is unholy. Does the unholy then become holy? We know the answer is no. If someone unclean touches something else, does that make that other thing unclean also? The answer is yes. The meaning is simple; holiness does not come about by contact with something holy. The holy rituals that the Israelites were performing in the past were not enough. Their disobedience and their ungodliness had contaminated everything they did. They may have had a wonderful Temple, once it was rebuilt, but if what is offered in the centre of it is unclean, then it must be consecrated again. The Temple had to be built; the community had to rededicate themselves to God. Judah could not be restored from exile unless they put God at the heart of their lives.

Finally, Haggai points us to the future in Haggai 2:20–23. He tells Zerubbabel that God will overthrow the nations and kingdoms of this world. Has this happened yet? No, so God must be referring to the last days. Zerubbabel was in the direct line of David and will become like God's signet ring. God has restored the monarchy and kept His promise from 2 Samuel 7:16. God reminds the people that they are His people.

Haggai teaches us that God expects us to live for Him, put Him first. There is a clear illustration in chapter 1 when we see the contrast between God's house and the people's houses. God asks them a direct and pointed question (Hag. 1:4). The people are challenged about spending money on decorating their houses but leaving God's house in ruins. This is a lesson for us today. We have to be careful not to spend all our time and money on what we want. We also need to dedicate time at the centre of our lives for God.

God also expects us to obey Him. God would have brought a drought if they had not done as He asked. If they obeyed, God would bless them according to the covenant He had with them. But if they disobeyed, the blessing could be withheld and things could get worse.

This book focuses on restoration with the rebuilding of the Temple. The people have returned from exile although many other Jewish people were scattered across the Babylonian Empire. They had lost their land, monarchy, Temple and religious lives. They must have wondered about how God was going to keep His promise that He made to Abraham in Genesis 12:1–3. God had promised them that they would return from exile.[3] Ezra and Nehemiah were given permission to return to Jerusalem, to rebuild the walls of the city and the Temple.[4] Queen Esther pleaded for the life of her countrymen to the king of Persia and succeeded.[5] Now they are back in their land and need to get things right this time. They have a second chance to put God at the heart of their nation.

With God's help, the walls are rebuilt, the Temple is rebuilt and community is thriving. God expects nothing less than their faithfulness. This is a new beginning with a new culture of faithfulness and obedience to God. They are a community of hope in the future, hope in a Messiah who will finally rescue them.

## About prayer

How can we use this to help shape our prayers? One of the things that stood out for me was the time and place that these people found themselves in.

Through the collapse of Israel, the Jewish people have been shown that they can worship God wherever they are – whether it was Daniel in Babylon, or Nehemiah in the ruins. We, too, are reminded that we can pray and worship God wherever we find ourselves. We do not need to scrub up, sitting on a pew on a Sunday morning at 11.05 a.m. We can be in a foreign land, heading into work at 7.30 a.m. on the local bus service. We can pray wherever we are, and whenever, to a God who listens to every word we utter.

We are also reminded that we all need a space that is dedicated to God at the centre of our lives. We also need to reorder our lives, ensuring that everything is in the right place. Sometimes family, work, money, or health take the place of God. We can even make them idols – worshipping our husbands, our loved ones, loving our leisure and pleasure more than time with God.

We also need a rhythm of prayer that is central to what we do; one that includes the business of our days, but also those intentional quiet times with God. We need to adopt rhythms and patterns in prayer that support our daily existence, direct our decisions and feed us. We were created to have an intimate relationship with God that is renewed and strengthened by prayer. This may include those fixed times of the day when we centre ourselves on God.

> In the morning, LORD, you hear my voice; in the morning I lay my requests before you and wait expectantly.
>
> *Ps. 5:3*

> On my bed I remember you; I think of you through the watches of the night.
>
> *Ps. 63:6*

> Very early in the morning, while it was still dark, Jesus got up, left the house and went off to a solitary place, where he prayed.
>
> *Mark 1:35*

> After he had dismissed them, he went up on a mountainside by himself to pray. Later that night, he was there alone'.
>
> *Matt. 14:23*

I have this picture of a huge marquee. It's probably because we have been looking at them for a November wedding! You can put all the other poles up, insert guy ropes (even the flashing luminous ones you now get) and the ground sheet, but if you don't have the right pole in the centre, it will not stand. It will collapse when a blast of wind comes. God needs to be at the centre of our lives. He should be our strength. We can try loads of other things, or allow them to push God out of the way, but only God will hold us up.

The people of Judah watched as their sister nation was torn apart and then fought off so many invaders and found their cities besieged. These were bloody, harsh, cruel times. Their armies would have died by the sword or survived war wounds that maimed their bodies and spirit. Ruined walls would have had to be constantly rebuilt. Eventually the people of Judah, too, were destroyed; the centre of their religious life was torn down and ransacked. They themselves were scattered across the huge Babylonian Empire.

Perhaps you feel like the Israelites: the years have taken their toll; every day is a battle; God is not listening. I am sure there are times when you just don't 'feel' like praying. But keep those appointments. We all need a timetable, a structure or a rhythm to our days. The American entrepreneur, motivational speaker and author Jim Rohn said, 'Either you run the day, or the day runs you'.[6] Psychologists suggest that successful people understand the importance of a timetable to their day, a routine or a rhythm that helps keep them focused. These people maximise their productivity, and this also enhances their wellbeing. In their book, *Common Prayer*, the writers Shane Claiborne, Jonathan Wilson-Hartgrove and Enuma Okoro say, 'Sometimes all you have to do is show up.'[7] Keep to your routine; things will change. Keep prayer a central part of your day.

The Israelites allowed their culture to change them. They shifted their focus off God and did their own thing. God had given laws and rules to help them live a flourishing life, and they rejected them. They lived according to their own drumbeat, forgetting God's heart. God, however, restored them and gave them a second chance. He does this for us too. "'I have chosen you," declares the LORD Almighty' (Hag. 2:23). 'The LORD of hosts' (ESV), the 'GOD-of-the-Angel-Armies' (MSG) has our back. Even when things change around us or we feel weighed down with life, we need to turn to God – He listens.

The Israelites responded to Haggai's first message (see Hag. 1) to rebuild the Temple, but they fretted about what they had achieved. It was never going to be like Solomon's Temple. God accepted what they had done, even though it was not an elaborate Temple, and He gave a value to it that it didn't naturally have.

We might not think we can achieve anything, that our prayers don't count. We need to trust that God uses what we give Him and gives it everlasting value. Pray when you don't feel like it, even if there are long silences; pray when you don't have the words. God is listening.

**Let's pray**

Father God,
We know that we let things crowd into our lives and take
    Your place.
We are sorry for how we have let that happen.
Help us to put You first.
We know that there are times when we don't know what to
    say; we don't have the words.
Help us to trust You.
In Jesus' name.
Amen.

# 12
# Malachi

# A Message of Hope

We have journeyed several hundred years through the lives of the people of Israel, the northern and southern kingdoms, and have heard the words of the minor prophets. Finally we come to Malachi, the last book of the Old Testament. Malachi was probably a contemporary of Nehemiah. He is considered one of the later prophets alongside Haggai and Zechariah.[1] More than 85 per cent of the book is attributed to God speaking directly to His people. The people thought God was silent and needed to hear His voice. The message is no different from the previous books. God reminds the people that He is their God. He reminds His people how they should live, that one day there will be a judgment– the wicked will be punished, the godly blessed. A fitting summary to the journey we have been on.

### The main character

We don't know much about the prophet Malachi. There is even some question that Malachi was a pen name for the prophet Ezra. Certainly, each prophet has shown their characteristics in their writing, and Malachi seems to be unique. In Malachi 1:1 he simply says, 'A prophecy: the word of the LORD to Israel through Malachi.' There is no mention of who his father is, no mention of his lineage or where he comes from. His name means 'messenger' and that appears fitting after hearing that so much of his book consists of direct words from God.

Although Malachi does not date his words like Haggai does, Malachi uses the Persian word for governor. This helps us identify that the time period must be between 538–333BC, when the Persian Empire ruled the Promised Land. Malachi also gives us other clues to his timeframe as he writes about corruption of the Temple sacrifices. This means that his message must have been delivered after the Israelites rebuilt the Temple in 515BC. His language and themes are like that of Nehemiah. It is therefore suggested that Malachi prophesied to the people around 432BC while he was God's spokesperson and while Nehemiah was on other business out of the city (Neh. 13:6). Malachi was probably prophesying in Jerusalem around 430BC, 100 years after the remnant returned to Judah from Babylon. Others have suggested that it was around 433–420BC.[2] Either way it was about a hundred years after the return from exile.

We have already heard about the governor Zerubbabel, who led the first group of exiles from Persia to their home in 537BC. A second group of people were led from exile to Judah by the prophet Ezra in 458BC. Then in 445BC Nehemiah led a third group of exiles back home. Through their leadership and others, the Temple had also been rebuilt.[3] The culture of worship and sacrifice had been established. This is only 100 years after the drama of escape and homecoming. God had given them a second chance, but the people blew it!

After only one or two generations the Jewish people had forgotten the difficult and painful lessons of what had happened in their past. You can hardly forget the destruction of a nation

and its cultural and religious heart, the capture and imprison-
ment of its people and then release of those people, the long
journeys home. How could you forget that the Lord has given
you a second chance?

In Malachi we learn that they have forgotten their past. The
heart of their faith at the centre of their community was again
corrupt, as the priests despised God, even offering blemished
animals in sacrifice. The people have turned away from God.
Their hearts are reflected in their actions; they have stopped
giving their tithes to God.

## The background

The book can be split into three sections. Section one is chapter
1:1–5 when the prophet reminds the people of God's unfailing
love. The second section, in chapter 1:6 – 2:17, is an accusation against the priest and the people for their spiritual decline
and apathy. Finally, chapters 3 – 4 are a reminder that God
does not change. One day, He will judge the guilty; one day,
He will bless the godly. Strong words which close the pages of
the Old Testament books.

Malachi lists six disputes or accusations that God has with His
people or they have with Him. It is like a game of ping pong –
God says something; the people respond. The people make an
accusation; God replies. Backwards and forwards they go until
the final and telling question: 'Is it worth it – serving God?' How
can they ask that after all they have gone through? They have
1,000 years of history from Abraham, a covenant from God and
the words of the prophets. Malachi answers them. The very first
words God wants His people to know are that He loves them.

- The first dispute – the people were questioning God's love for them. He compares what He has done for Edom and Judah. He tells them in Malachi 1:2, 'I have loved you . . . But you ask, "How have you loved us?" Was not Esau Jacob's brother? . . . Yet I have loved Jacob . . .'
- The second dispute is God accusing the priests of not honouring God (Mal. 1: 6–9).
- The third dispute is God condemning the people for worshipping other gods and not keeping God's law about issues such as divorce (Mal. 2:10–16).
- The fourth dispute is about God's justice. The people were asking, 'Where is the God of justice?' (Mal. 2:17).
- The fifth dispute is a call for repentance. A sign of this would be that the people reinstate their tithes (Mal. 3:6–12).
- The sixth dispute is about the cost of servicing God. The people ask the question, 'What do we gain by carrying out [God's] requirements . . .?' (Mal. 3:14).

Despite this last question, God still says, in Malachi 3:17, 'they will be my treasured possession'. The book ends with Malachi 4 and a message about the 'day of the LORD' (Mal. 4:5,6).

### The main message

Like the books of Haggai and Zechariah, Malachi was written to the Jewish people post exile. These books contained messages of hope to a remnant of people finding their feet in a new world. The biblical texts tell the story of a discouraged and demoralised people. Ezra informs us that the initial remnant of people who returned to Judah were 42,360, as well as 7,337 slaves and 200 singers.[4] They returned to rebuild the ruins of houses, cities and cultivate the land. This would have been a tough project. How do you rebuild a city that has been torn down?

After the liberation of Paris from the Nazis during the Second World War, food was becoming scarcer by the day. The French rail network had largely been destroyed, so transporting food into Paris was a problem. The Germans had stripped the capital of all its rich resources. The Allies had to import up to 2,400 tons of food per day. Refugees had to reunite with families that had been forcibly torn apart. The scale of the task was enormous. This was because most of the ports in Europe and Asia had been destroyed, bridges had been blown up, railway stock had vanished. Great cities such as Paris and Berlin were piles of rubble. It took years, decades, to rebuild things, and that was with the knowledge and equipment they had in the 1940–60s. Rebuilding and restoration is a huge undertaking at any time – no wonder the Jewish people were discouraged.

## About prayer

I think what stood out for me when reading this book was that we pray to an unchanging God. Malachi can encourage us by its main themes of love and hope.

The first theme is that God is unchanging. The children of Israel had been taught this through the centuries of their history. God is merciful, He loves His children. Malachi 3:6 says, 'I the LORD do not change. So you, the descendants of Jacob, are not destroyed.' Throughout the book, we have heard all the accusations that are made, but God remains true to His character.

He starts by telling Israel how much they are loved. We can approach God in prayer knowing that we are loved. We may make repeated mistakes, but He forgives us, and we can have confidence that He forgives us. God forgave Israel on numerous occasions, and they have the confidence to approach God. How much more confidence should we have as Jesus intercedes for us on our behalf? In Hebrews 7:23–26 we are told:

> Now there have been many of those priests, since death prevented them from continuing in office; but because Jesus lives for ever, he has a permanent priesthood. Therefore he is able to save completely those who come to God through him, because he always lives to intercede for them. Such a high priest truly meets our need – one who is holy, blameless, pure, set apart from sinners, exalted above the heavens.

Another theme is that God is a righteous God. God's heart must have broken on so many occasions because of Israel's treatment of Him. His people, whom He clearly loved, neglected Him. They even brought sacrifices that were blemished and didn't pay their tithes, as we are told in Malachi 1:6:

> 'A son honours his father, and a slave his master. If I am a father, where is the honour due to me? If I am a master, where is the re-spect due to me?' says the LORD Almighty.
>   'It is you priests who show contempt for my name.
>   'But you ask, "How have we shown contempt for your name?"'

We are never going to be perfect, but we can bring our best to God. When we pray, let's give Him the honour that He is due. Show respect, give Him time.

Finally, God is our judge. In Malachi 4:1 we read:

> 'Surely the day is coming; it will burn like a furnace. All the ar-rogant and every evildoer will be stubble, and that day that is coming will set them on fire,' says the LORD Almighty. 'Not a root or a branch will be left to them.'

There are a few simple lessons that we can take from this book. They are as follows:

- God loves us.
- Respect God and His law.
- Consider God's justice.
- Give God what He is due.
- Remember that there will be a day of judgment.

Throughout the history of Israel, we see that they failed again and again. They rejected God, were apathetic to His law and forgot His promises. Again and again, God sent words to remind them that they were loved (Mal. 1:2). We have seen in the previous books that Israel would fail, prompting the cycle to begin again. God's final word to His people is a message of judgment for sin. The book ends with a 'curse', followed by 400 years of silence. The New Testament speaks of grace. The next words are the genealogy of Jesus in Matthew 1. This time God did not send another prophet – He sent His Son.

## Let's pray

Father,
Thank you that we can turn to You even though we fail again and again.
Thank You that You love us with an everlasting love.
Thank You that You never turn us away.
Thank You that we can look to You because of what Jesus has done.
Through His name.
Amen.

# The Final Word

# In the Light of a Pandemic

I started this book saying that as a family in the past few years we have had some interesting challenges around loss and grief. During times of deep emotion, we have turned again and again to God with our petitions and in prayers of lament. Sometimes we have not been able to verbalise how we feel but have echoed the words of the psalmist or the minor prophets as we have navigated some deep valleys and high mountains. I have found solace in these places.

As I have journeyed through the night of grief into morning, these passages of Scripture have become more precious to me. I find that I am now having to process the sheer impact of Covid-19. I have had to turn to God as I have tried to cope with living during a pandemic. The verses that I have digested over the last few months are brought back to remembrance by God's Spirit. He has become my place of refuge and safety. I am not hiding out in a high tower but can look over the plains in front of me. I am impacted by the pain this virus has brought. I have spent every night during isolation with my brothers and sisters online from around the world praying for the current situation. I have prayed more during this period than at any other time in my life. I do not admit to being an expert on prayer, but I do know who I am praying to.

In December 2019 information was released about an infectious disease in China that seemed to be spreading like wildfire. On 11 February 2020, the International Committee on Taxonomy of viruses announced that the virus was called the 'severe acute respiratory syndrome coronavirus 2 (SARS-CoV-2) and the disease became known as coronavirus or Covid-19. The first confirmed case in the UK was 31 January 2020. On 11 March 2020, the World Health Organization (WHO) announced that it was deemed a pandemic.[1] I had finished the manuscript and we were entering unprecedented times coping with the implications of a pandemic. As I write, the death rate in the UK has surpassed 40,000 and is nearer 50,000 with disputes over the true death figure. Globally there have been approximately 800,000 deaths and the death rate keeps rising. Some countries are experiencing a second wave of the disease.

I had been at home shielding for twelve weeks due to having brittle asthma. That means I had to stay at home and not go outside apart from to exercise. Now, I am beginning to step out into this different world. My day-to-day life has changed, and the world around me is in a period of mourning and lament. Many people across the world have experienced things they have not experienced before.

My dad has end-stage Alzheimer's disease and is in a care home. My mum, who visited Dad every day, cannot see him as his home is locked down and no one can visit. Mum is at home alone, missing Dad. I also miss my son and his wife and my new little grandson, Arthur, who was born the week before lockdown. We were so fortunate we got to see him in his first week of life, but I have no idea when I will see them again. My son, who is at home with us, cannot visit his fiancée. They do not know how this will affect their wedding plans. One of our daughters is back from university and is now a front-line worker so we must keep apart in the home – I cannot even hug her. This is challenging for all types of people – from those who are single and living alone to those worried about their health with terminal cancer.

It is so hard to know how to support and care for the people that we know and love. I have had friends who have been in hospital fighting this virus, and others who are grieving the loss of loved ones. I have friends and family who are front-line staff coping with the reality that they, too, can catch this virus; they, too, are at risk.

This is just my story. I have read of so many families coping with huge strains due to the pandemic, and awful situations – whole families ripped apart with grief as children are orphaned and families struggle with this deadly virus. These days will be recorded in the annals of history. We may have never journeyed this way before, but nothing is a surprise to God. The last time there was a significant pandemic was the Spanish Flu outbreak in 1918.

The 1918–19 influenza pandemic started just as the First World War was ending. It is thought that as many as 50 million people died worldwide because of it, more than twice as many as the number killed in the war. More died in a single year of the Spanish Flu pandemic than died in the four years of the Black Death from 1347–51. Many of the people who died were young adults age 20 to 40 who had no immunity from previous strains of influenza. Not only was 1918 the last year of the First World War, but in the aftermath of war there was economic hardship and rationing. There was also a global shortage of doctors and nurses, many still on the battlefields across Europe, coping with the injured soldiers. People campaigned across the country to raise money for the war effort. Influenzae swept through many malnourished and weary people, killing all ages. My own great-grandmother Rachel died during the pandemic of Spanish Flu.

Death and dying had become ingrained in the culture, as families still dealing with bereavement from the war saw family members die within days of the first symptoms of the flu. As the death toll rose, undertakers could not keep up with demands. Eventually families had to even dig their own relatives' graves. There were shortages of coffins and funerals were limited to fifteen minutes each as bodies piled up in the morgues.[2]

During the pandemic, churches were also closed from early autumn through to Armistice day in the November. In hindsight they opened up too early in the pandemic. Local newspapers offered to print sermons, passages of Scripture and church announcements if they were sent in by the local clergy, to help people worship at home. We are fortunate to have online resources. For the past sixty nights my husband has broadcast a live prayer time on Facebook called 'Nite prayer'. I have either been involved in answering comments or been involved in the live prayers. The pages of this book have become a living reality as I have read the prayers and messages from people all over the world. They are beautiful, poignant and even breath-taking. It is an honour to be a part of these prayer times. Sometimes I feel I am listening into the most intimate and beautiful of conversations.

Justin Welby, the Archbishop of Canterbury, tells us, 'Prayer is one of the most intimate and beautiful activities in which human beings can engage, whether alone or with others.' He goes on to say, 'When we pray, we participate in the most dramatic partnership of creation and recreation.'[3] We are in partnership with God – we are changed, and the world around us is changed.

Yesterday I asked myself, 'What do I know about prayer?' A strange question at the end of a book. My response are the words of Pete Grieg, the founder of the 24–7 prayer movement, at the start of his book, *How to Pray*. Pete tells us that although most people pray, no one finds it easy. We actually all need a little help to pray as no one is perfect.[4]

I think that is so true. No one finds it easy. It is strange, as prayer is one of the most important aspects of our spiritual lives. Ultimately, we only learn to pray by participating in this conversation with God, by praying. It is like any skill – we can read all the books, watch loads of online sermons and podcasts, but we only learn how to do it by doing it ourselves. Sometimes we don't pray, as we just do not know where to begin. We know what we want to pray about, but we do not know how to start. I must admit, I read the comments on my husband's prayer feed during 'Nite prayer' and sometimes the words are lost in the mix of emotion.

What do we say or how do we start to pray? During 'Nite prayer' we often say the Lord's Prayer together to help us focus our prayer time:

> Father,
> hallowed be your name,
> your kingdom come.
> Give us each day our daily bread.
> Forgive us our sins,
> for we also forgive everyone who sins against us.
> And lead us not into temptation.

*Luke 11:2–4*

I also think, for some, it is easy to pray when things are going well. We can thank and praise God for all manner of things. It is tough when we do not know what to say, when things are confusing, or we are standing on the precipice of something frightening. The lesson is that I can pray even when I feel like this.

The other lesson I have learned is that I need to still my mind and sit in God's presence in silence. If we read the noisy, challenging, poetic psalms we may come across the word or exclamation 'Selah' in some versions of the Bible, such as the ESV. It is also found in the book of Habakkuk and is possibly a musical direction. No one really know what it means – perhaps it is an instruction to pause. In fact, in the Septuagint, the earliest Greek translation of the Old Testament, it is translated as 'intermission'. We all need to pause; we all need to stop and just be. That may seem strange – when we feel we need to keep praying, keep doing something. We do, however, need to stop, to pause and gain strength from God. We can sit in comfortable silence, just like my times during the long car journeys with my husband.

While at home during the period of lockdown, my daughter and I have been doing an intense exercise regime. Every few days we have a rest day when we do not do squats, planks, jumping jacks. You can tell I do not usually do these things. I much prefer going to the gym, plugging in my headphones to watch TV, and using their equipment. I have felt guilty having a day off. It is, however, important to have a rest day during any exercise regimen or plan. Exercise depletes your muscles' glycogen levels, which are stores of energy. If these stores are not replaced, we experience muscle fatigue and soreness. We can get fatigued for lots of other reasons.

Compassion fatigue is one type of fatigue and is characterised by emotional and physical exhaustion which leads to a reduced ability to empathise or feel compassion for others.

Compassion can be defined as a deep awareness of the suffering of others alongside a wish to help relieve it. People can develop this type of fatigue when working directly with victims who undergo trauma, or illness. It is something I, as a nurse and working in health care, have been aware of through the years. It is certainly something front-line workers may experience in the shadows of Covid-19. One of the coping strategies to prevent it is time out, ensuring health care workers have time to pause, even in the middle of a pandemic. During our prayer times we sometimes just stop, gain strength from God, and allow Him to minister to all those online.

I have also been amazed by the fact that so many people are praying. There are people who have joined us who do not go to church or have not prayed before. According to a recent poll commissioned by Tearfund, one in twenty British adults say they have started praying during the lockdown, when they did not pray before the pandemic.[5] The online poll was carried out between 24–27 April as the cases and death rate of Covid-19, a few weeks after the peak, had levelled off. More people in Britain are turning to prayer, and nearly a quarter of people have watched or listened to an online church service since the lockdown began on the 23 March 2020, when church buildings closed to public services. There appear to be fewer religious boundaries; simply people scared, mourning, or in loss, wanting to talk to God. Many people who have never really prayed before are joining us or other people, online, in their homes. They are finding spaces to talk with God, to engage with Him, sharing their fears and concerns in unprecedented times. In fact, the Church of England reported 6,000 people phoned a prayer hotline in its first forty-eight hours of operation.[6]

The Israelites are famous for turning to God after they exhausted all other options. We are no different today. Clearly, that is not what God wants – to be treated as an afterthought.

We fail to make God a priority. Nothing takes God by surprise and He misses nothing. Sometimes we forget that.

The words of the minor prophets, however, remind us of the character of God. He has not forgotten us. He calls us to repentance, but also points us forward to a day of hope when He will dwell with His people again. God's steadfast love never gives up. God promises to take the people at their point of need and transform their troubles into an opportunity to understand His blessing. We are also reminded of God's faithfulness. It is the faithfulness of God in the past that allows Habakkuk to rejoice during a difficult time in their history. As God was with the people of Israel in the past, He is with us now:

> Though the fig-tree does not bud and there are no grapes on the vines, though the olive crop fails and the fields produce no food, though there are no sheep in the sheepfold and no cattle in the stalls, yet I will rejoice in the LORD, I will be joyful in God my Saviour.
>
> *Hab. 3:17,18*

I asked people on social media what they felt they had learned about prayer during this pandemic. Several people told me that they knew they were not alone – they were a part of a larger community; they said that their boundaries have changed – they had learned to look beyond themselves. Others simply told me that they should have been praying more and that it was not as hard as they thought it would be.

I think the deepest lesson I have learned is not profound, nor is it a 'bolt of lightning' moment. It is that He is here, and I can simply be. There are days when I have words and days when God's Spirit intervenes for me. We may think we need the right words, the ability to pray lengthy, wordy prayers.

Instead, I have learned to sit in silence to ask the Spirit to guide my words. When we do not have the words to say, the Spirit intercedes on our behalf. The Spirit also gives us the strength to talk to God when we do not feel like praying at all. In Romans 8:26,27 we read:

> In the same way, the Spirit helps us in our weakness. We do not know what we ought to pray for, but the Spirit himself intercedes for us through wordless groans. And he who searches our hearts knows the mind of the Spirit, because the Spirit intercedes for God's people in accordance with the will of God.

Some reminded me recently of the words of a song by Matt Redman called the 'Heart of Worship' (When the Music Fades). There is a line in it which asks us what we can do if everything is pulled back to expose what is beneath. It feels like everything is stripped back. No normal work patterns, no meetings with friends and going to church services. No large meetings with uplifting music and praise. Instead, I feel it has all been stripped away – it's just me laid bare in front of God. That can be scary. How do we approach the throne of the highest, the One who made the stars in the sky and shifted the seas with one word? His love holds me, captivates me, and allows me to be me, sitting in His presence. I do not need to know which words to say – He even helps me with that.

The situation that I am living through is so unique. It feels like the world has paused for a while. I look at pictures of Trafalgar Square – quiet, apart from the odd pigeon; or the Canals of Venice, which has swapped gondolas for dolphins.

The Revd Fletcher Parrish was pastor of Eleventh Avenue Methodist Church during the 1918 Spanish Flu pandemic in

Birmingham, USA. His sermon was printed in the local paper. He said:

> Meditation is very profitable for the soul, but the rush of the world is so great at present that very little time is given to cogitation and reflection. Men think they have no time to walk out in the fields for contemplation, or to sit quietly by the fireside and muse. However, we have a God-given opportunity for this helpful indulgence by reason of this unique Sabbath which has dawned upon us. Out of necessity our churches are closed, and all public gatherings must be discontinued. We cannot go motoring, and we would not go to business if we could, and even the fields are dangerous lest we should meet goldenrod and ragweed and take influenza. But we can sit by the fire and give ourselves to thought and reflection which will bring great profit to us.[7]

Interestingly, Rabbi Emanu-El Rabbi Morris Newfield, a prominent reformer of his day, writing in the paper during the 1918 pandemic said of the climate of the day that it gives people a better understanding of God.[8] Reflecting on these past events have reminded us that God does not change. The words of the minor prophets can also speak into our situation today. Their lament over Israel can become our own lament.

# Appendix

# The World Prayer Centre[1]

The World Prayer Centre is a charitable organisation with a few simple aims. These are to inform, enable and empower others in prayer and worship. They have a networking role working with a range of people and nations bringing people together to pray. They also have a building based in Birmingham where they host national prayer events.

They feel their calling is to be 'a house of prayer for all nations' (Isa. 56:7). They are shaped by three core aims:

- Heaven to earth – being directed by God and not human beings.
- The importance of the cross – underscoring the power of Jesus dying on the cross.
- The Word and Spirit – being guided by the Scriptures, which should also encourage us how we should pray.

**The story of the journey to date of a World Prayer Centre vision**

In 1992 God gave Ian Cole a vision for a World Prayer Centre. He impressed on Ian a vision to see established in the heart of the nation a Christian centre that both in its design and purpose enabled people to pray, act, learn and share something of God's kingdom at a local, national and global level. It started while Ian was sitting in a very wet tent on holiday in the middle of France reading the story of Nehemiah. These are Ian's words:

> As I read the account of his building programme of walls, gates and towers, I pondered on the necessity and purpose of the towers. They were high places from which watchmen, the seers, could observe what was going on in the city and more importantly give warning to what was coming against the city from outside forces, be it good for the city and its people, or evil and destructive. My second prompting came as I read Isaiah 56. Here the prophet is speaking God's word concerning maintaining justice, doing what is right, keeping the Sabbath, refraining from evil. My third prompting came from Isaiah 58.
>
> My immediate challenge was how to respond to these promptings! Were these thoughts of a prayer tower, prayer centre, from the Lord? Was this a fanciful holiday idea, had the rain affected my brain? It could not be said that prayer was at the top of most Christians' agenda. Mission and evangelism was, Christian social action was, church planting was being mentioned, but most churches in the 1990s did not even have a prayer meeting, and yet here in God's word, and later quoted by Jesus, God was saying, 'My house shall be called a house of prayer for all nations' (Isa: 56:7, NKJV.) I could see a place that in its purpose and structure demonstrated God's kingdom, 'a house of prayer for all nations'.

Months rolled into years and nothing seemed to be moving. Then two remarkable things happened. My wife, Pauline, and I felt we should attend a conference in London at which Julie Anderson and Cindy Jacobs were speaking. We arrived late and were sitting on the back row when suddenly this lady, who turned out to be Cindy Jacobs, came and grabbed our arms, took us to the front and prophesied that the vision God had given us for a centre for prayer would, in His time, come about, and she also described things that had been on my soggy papers that no one had ever seen!

Sometime later I was helping to lead a prayer conference at The Hayes Conference Centre Swanwick. Standing next to me on the platform was the Revd Bob Dunnett, a spiritual father to us and many others. To my shock and, I have to say, horror, he asked me to share the World Prayer Centre vision. They were so supportive of this vision and God used them to help me.

So, in 1997, World Prayer Centre became a registered charity. There was a lot to do, but with God's help, the team that God put together did it! Seeing what God was doing in these places simply emphasised the growing belief in us that prayer in all its forms, be it liturgical, spontaneous, meditative, spiritual warfare, in private or in public, is the key to see the kingdom of God come on earth as in heaven. In place after place we saw that, as people surrendered their agendas to God, confessed the sin of disunity and came together in humility to seek His face, there He commanded His blessing (see Ps. 133), the church grew and communities were transformed.

Over the years we have found ourselves in the United Nations with teams praying through Global issues. We have travelled with others to be where the G8 leaders met to pray for God's will to be done through them. In 2003 we were invited to the launch of the International Prayer Council, a fellowship of national prayer leaders representing every continent of the world. Several global events have seen many thousands gathering together, including the 2012 World Prayer assembly at which over nine thousand delegates, representing eighty-five nations, gathered in Indonesia to launch a 'New Wave' of prayer that continues to break in many nations. Over the years, thousands have gathered in arenas in Birmingham as, in obedience and faith to that call, we have blown the trumpet, worshipped God and prayed for His sovereignty to be seen over the nation.

For more information about the World Prayer Centre please visit: https://www.worldprayer.org.uk.

# Notes

## Introduction

1   S. Robson, 'Six of the World's Seven Billion People Have Mobile Phones . . . But Only 4.5 Billion Have a Toilet says UN Report, https://www.dailymail.co.uk/news/article-2297508/Six-world-s-seven-billion-people-mobile-phones--4-5 billion-toilet-says-UN-report.html (accessed 2 September 2020).

2   C. Warren, 'Average Internet User Now Spends 68 hours Per Month Online', https://mashable.com/2009/10/14/net-usage-nielsen/?europe=true

3   E. Bernstein, 2011 'Your Blackberry or Your Wife', *The Wall Street Journal D1 & D4* Last accessed 28/08/2020 http://on.wsj.com/gXASsx.

4   Catechism of the Catholic Church 2590, ttp://www.vatican.va/archive/ccc_css/archive/catechism/p4s1c1a1.htm (accessed 28 August 2020).

5   Pierre Descouvemont, Helmuth Nils Loose, (1996). *Thérèse and Lisieux*. Toronto: Novalis. p. 5.

6   J. Mazarin, 'Why does prayer sometimes feel so boring?', https://relevantmagazine.com/god/why-does-prayer-sometimes-feel-so-boring (accessed 1 August 2020).

7   R. Alter, *Genesis: Translation and Commentary* (NY: W.W. Norton & Company, 1997), p. x; T. Longman III, *How to Read Genesis*

(Westmont, IL: IVP, 2009); T. Thompson, *The Bible in History: How Writers Create a Past.* (Bournemouth: Pimilico, 1999).

8   1 Pet. 1:20; Rev. 13:8.

9   Menachem Posner, 'Who Was Abraham? The First Patriarch in the Bible', https://www.chabad.org/library/article_cdo/aid/112356/ jewish/Who-Was-Abraham-The-First-Patriarch-in-the-Bible.htm (accessed 1 August 2020).

10  1 Kgs 11,12.

11  W.G. Dever, *What Did the Biblical Writers Know & When Did They Know It? What Archeology Can Tell Us about the Reality of Ancient Israel* (Grand Rapids, MI: Eerdmans, 2001,) p. 10.

12  G. Smith, *Interpreting the Prophetic Books* (ed. D. Howard Jr; Grand Rapids, MI: Kregel Academic, 2012).

13  The law-suit speech was first suggested by H. Gunkel in 1923. H.F. Hahn, *The Old Testament in Modern Research* (London: SCM Press, 1956), pp. 119–28.

14  D.R. Daniels, 'Is There a prophetic Lawsuit' *Zeitschrift für die alttestamentliche Wissenschaft* 99 (3) (1987) pp. 339–60.

15  C. Sinclair. 2008. *The Hitch-Hiker's Guide to the Bible* (Oxford: Monarch Books).

# 1 Jonah   When Things Don't Go Our Way

1   R.E. Clements, *The Purpose of the Book of Jonah*, Congress Volume (Edinburgh: 1974), pp. 16–28.

2   C. Sinclair, *The Hitch-Hiker's Guide to the Bible* (Oxford: Monarch Books, 2008).

3   J.H. Gaines, 'Forgiveness in a Wounded World: Jonah's Dilemma', Society of Biblical Literature (No. 5), 2003.

4   E.R. Thiele, *The Mysterious Numbers of the Hebrew Kings* (3rd ed.; Grand Rapids, MI: Zondervan/Kregel, 1983), p. 217.

5   A.J. Wilson, 1927, *Princeton Theological Review*, XXV, October 1927, https://archive.org/stream/princetontheolog2541arms/ princetontheolog2541arms_djvu.txt (accessed 1 September 2020).

6   B. Shattuck, 'Swallowed by a Whale – a true tale?', https://www. salon.com/2012/01/15/swallowed_by_a_whale_a_true_tale/ (accessed 1 August 2020).

7   S.B. Noegel, 'Jonah and Leviathan' *Henoch 37* (2), 2015.

8   C. Lewis, Jonah – A Parable for Our Time, *Judaism, 21*(2), 15 January 2012, p. 159.

9   T.E. Fretheim, 'Jonah and theodicy' *Zeitschrift für die alttestamentliche Wissenschaft 90* (2), 1978, pp. 227–37.

10  Gaines, 'Forgiveness in a Wounded World: Jonah's Dilemma'.

11  T.E. Fretheim, T. E, 'The Exaggerated God of Jonah', *Word and World 27* (2), p. 125, 2007.

12  R.B. Scott, 'The Sign of Jonah: An Interpretation' *Union Seminary Magazine 19* (1), 1965, pp.16–25.

13  F.N.M. Diekstra, 'Jonah and Patience: The Psychology of a Prophet' *English Studies 55* (3), 1974, pp. 205–17.

14  E.T. Welch, *When People Are Big and God Is Small* (Phillipsburg, NJ: Presbyterian and Reformed Publishing Company, 1997).

15  F.B. Jevons. *An Introduction to the Study of Comparative Religion* (New York: The Macmillan Company, 1908), p. 73.

16  Heb. 4:14; 4:16.

## 2  Amos   A Cry for Justice  *Anna Arnold*

1   Ps. 103:6.

2   Amos 2:7; 5:7; 5:10; 5:12; 5:15; 5:24; 6:12.

3   Zech. 14:5.

4   Pseudonym. It would not be safe or fair to reveal more of Grace's identity.

5   Amos 1:3–5.

6   Amos 1:6–8.

7   Amos 1:9,10.

8   Amos 1:11,12.

9   Amos 1:13–15.

10  Amos 2:1–3.

11  Amos 2:4,5.

[12] Exod. 18.

[13] Amos 5:12.

[14] Tom Finley, 'Social Justice in Amos', https://www.biola.edu/blogs/good-book-blog/2015/social-justice-in-amos (accessed 1 August 2020).

[15] Amos 1:6–10.

[16] https://www.ijmuk.org (accessed 2 September 2020).

[17] Walk Free, 'Global Slavery Index', https://www.globalslaveryindex.org (accessed 1 August 2020).

[18] T. Keller, *Generous Justice* (London: Hodder & Stoughton 2012), p. 51.

[19] Amos – the prophet and part-time shepherd from the southern kingdom who prophesied into the northern nation. He didn't exactly fit in, nor was he who you would expect to be a prophet.

[20] Amos 5:24.

[21] Amos 9:13.

## 3  Hosea   A Cry to Be Faithful  *Cathy Le Feuvre*

[1] A. Remmers, 'Book Overview – Hosea', https://www.studylight.org/commentaries/spe/hosea.html (accessed 1 August 2020).

[2] Hos. 1:3–9.

[3] R.L. Strauss, 'Underlying Love – The Story of Hosea and Gomer', https://bible.org/seriespage/8-undying-love-story-hosea-and-gomer (accessed 1 August 2020).

[4] F. Landy, *Hosea* (NY: Bloomsbury, 1995).

[5] Remmers, 'Book Overview – Hosea'.

[6] Gowans, Larssons, *Hosea*, http://www.gowans-larsson.com/Hosea/index.html (accessed 1 August 2020).

[7] Lieutenant-Colonel T. Davis. The Salvation Army Songbook No. 72 (UK: Salvation Army, 2015).

## 4 Nahum    Repentance

1   H.H. Halley, *Halley's Bible Handbook: An Abbreviated Bible Commentary* (Grand Rapids, MI: Zondervan, 24th edition, 1961), p. 368.

2   A.S. Van der Woude, 'The Book of Nahum: A Letter Written in Exile,' Joint British-Dutch Old Testament Conference (1976: Louvain, Belgium), *Instruction and Interpretation: Studies in Hebrew Language, Palestinian Archaeology and Biblical Exegesis* (ed. A.S. van der Woude; Leiden: E.J. Brill, 1977), pp. 108–26.

3   Maier, The Book of Nahum, pp. 27–40, 87–139; van Wyk, 'Allusions to "Prehistory" and History in the Book of Nahum', pp. 222–32; R.D. Patterson, *Nahum, Habakkuk, Zephaniah, The Wycliffe Exegetical Commentary* (Chicago, IL: Moody Press, 1980), pp. 3–7.

4   *The Scofield® Study Bible* (Oxford: Oxford University Press, 2003), pp. 1185–7.

5   O. Palmer Robertson, *The Books of Nahum, Habakkuk, and Zephaniah* (Grand Rapids, MI: Eerdmans, 1994).

6   J.R.R. Tolkien, *The Lord of the Rings* (London: HarperCollins, 1995).

7   J. Jones, 'Some of the Most Appalling Images Ever Created – I Am Ashurbanipal Review', https://www.theguardian.com/artand-design/2018/nov/06/i-am-ashurbanipal-review-british-museum (accessed 1 August 2020).

8   C. Sinclair, *The Hitch-Hiker's Guide to the Bible* (Oxford: Monarch Books, 2008), p. 115.

9   D. Baker, *Nahum, Habakkuk and Zephaniah, Tyndale Old Testament Commentaries* (Westmont, IL: IVP, 1985) p. 15.

10   2 Chr. 27.

11   See also Isaiah 7.

12   2 Kgs 20:20; 2 Chr. 32:30.

13   2 Kgs 18:15.

14 J-P. Isbouts,'Isaiah: the fiery prophet who saved Jerusalem' *National Geographic* https://www.nationalgeographic.co.uk/history-and-civilisation/2019/01/isaiah-fiery-prophet-who-saved-jerusalem (accessed 1 August 2020).

15 J.B. Pritchard, *Ancient Near Eastern Texts* (2nd edition Princeton) (Princeton, NJ: Princeton University Press, 1955), p. 287.

16 Isa. 37:36.

17 J. Bright, *A History of Israel* (Louisville: Westminster John Knox Press, 2000), p. 200.

18 2 Kgs 21.

19 The Temple was destroyed by the Romans in 70AD during the great siege of Jerusalem.

20 E. Harris, 'Do Mercy and Justice Contradict Each Other? Pope Francis Says No', https://www.catholicnewsagency.com/news/do-mercy-and-justice-contradict-each-other-pope-francis-says-no-75638 (accessed 1 August 2020).

21 Matt. 3:2.

22 'A Sermon (No. 1778). Preached on Wednesday Morning, April 30th, 1884, By C. H. SPURGEON, At Exeter-Hall Being the Annual Sermon of the Baptist Missionary Society', http://www.gospelweb.net/SpurgeonMTP30/spursermon1778.htm (accessed 17 September 2020).

23 Ibid.

24 J. Calvin, *Commentary on Matthew, Mark and Luke, Part 1* (London: Forgotten Books, 2007).

## 5 Micah   A Cry for Justice and Mercy

1 Mic. 1:1.

2 2 Kgs 15:33–35.

3 2 Kgs 16; Isa. 7,8.

4 Matt. 1:10.

5 G. Smith, *Interpreting the Prophetic Books* (ed. D. Howard Jr; Grand Rapids, MI: Kregel Academic, 2012), p. 77.

6 Micah 1:9.

[7]  B. Malchow, 'Social Justice in the Hebrew Bible: What Is New and What Is Old?' (Wilmington, DE: Michael Glazier Inc., 1996), pp. 48–52.

[8]  Claude Mariottini, 'Micah, the Prophet of the Poor', https://claudemariottini.com/2014/02/21/micah-the-prophet-of-the-poor (accessed 1 September 2020).

[9]  C.R. Swindoll, *A Life Well Lived* (Nashville, TN: Thomas Nelson, 2010).

[10]  W. VanGemeren, *Interpreting the Prophetic Word: An Introduction to the Prophetic Literature of the Old Testament.* (Grand Rapids, MI: Zondervan, 1996), p. 31.

[11]  N. Ruddock, 'How to Pray for Justice', https://www.worldprayer. org.uk/blog/how-to-pray-for-justice (accessed 1 September 2020).

# 6  Zephaniah    A Plea to God

[1]  J. Calvin, *Commentary on Habakkuk, Zephaniah, Haggai* (Grand Rapids, MI: Eerdmans, 1950), p. 2.

[2]  2 Kgs 22:3–10.

[3]  2 Kgs 21:16; 2 Chr. 33:1–10.

[4]  Calvin, *Commentary on Habakkuk, Zephaniah, Haggai.* p. 4.

[5]  F.C. Fensham, 'The Poetic Form of the Hymn of the Day of the Lord in Zephaniah', *OTWSA*, 14 (1) (1970), pp. 9–14.

[6]  R. Lowth, *Lectures on the Sacred Poetry of the Hebrews,* Vol. 2, No. 72 (St Paul's Church-Yard, 1839).

[7]  P.R. House, *Zephaniah: A Prophetic Drama*, Vol. 69 (Worcester: Sheffield Academic Press, 1989).

[8]  R.C. Sproul, *The Holiness of God* (Wheaton, IL: Tyndale House Publishers, 1997), p. 40.

[9]  Rom. 3:10.

[10]  M.A. Sweeney, *King Josiah of Judah* (Oxford: Oxford University Press, 2001), p. 137.

[11]  http://spurgeon.10000quotes.com/archives/293 (accessed 18 September 2020).

[12] The Charles Spurgeon sermon collection. https://www.theking-domcollective.com/spurgeon/sermon/101/ (accessed 17 September 2020).

[13] https://www.hymnal.net/en/hymn/h/290 (accessed 7 September 2020).

## 7 Habakkuk   Praise and Lament

[1] See Jer. 26:20–23.

[2] Warren Wiersbe, *From Worry to Worship* (La Vergne, TN: Spring Arbor Distributors, 1983)

[3] J.W. Watts, *Psalmody in Prophecy: Habakkuk 3 in context* (Sheffield: JSOT Press, 1996).

[4] G.T. Prinsloo, 'Yahweh the Warrior: An Intertextual Reading of Habakkuk 3', *Old Testament Essays*, 14 (3), 2001, pp. 475–93.

[5] K. Arnold, K. McDermott & D. Szpunar, 'Imagining the Near and Far Future: The Role of Location Familiarity', *Memory & Cognition*, Vol. 39 (6), 2008, pp. 954–67.

[6] J. Montgomery Boice, *The Minor Prophets*, Vol. 2 (Grand Rapids, MI: Kregal Publications, 1996), p. 110.

[7] R.P. Carroll, 'Habakkuk', in R.J. Coggins and J.L. Houlden (eds.), *A Dictionary of Biblical Interpretation* (London: SCM, 1990), p. 269.

[8] L. Boettner, *The Reformed Doctrine of Predestination* (Phillipsburg, NJ: Presbyterian and Reformed, 1932) p. 222.

[9] See https://www.csw.org.uk/prayforleah for more details.

[10] P. Miller, *A Praying Life*: Connecting with God in a Distracting World (Wheaton, IL: Tyndale House Publishers, 2017), Chapter 23.

[11] Miller, *A Praying Life*, Chapter 23.

[12] L. Huffman, 'Heart Sounds: Hear the Story', *Nursing Made Incredibly Easy!*, Vol. 10 (2), March/April 2012, pp. 51–4.

[13] S1 and S2 are terms used in medicine to describe the heart sounds.

## 8 Joel A Plea for Repentance

1 See European Centre for Disease Prevention and Control for up to date figures. https://www.ecdc.europa.eu/en/geographical-distribution-2019-ncov-cases (accessed 1 September 2020).

2 J. Grehan, *Twilight of the Saints: Everyday Religion in Ottoman Syria and Palestine* (Oxford: Oxford University Press, 2014), p. 1.

3 1 Chr. 4:35.

4 1 Chr. 5:12.

5 1 Chr. 11:38.

6 2 Chr. 29:12.

7 J. Calvin, *Commentary on Joel, Amos, Obadiah* (Grand Rapids, MI: Christian Classics Ethereal Library, 1999-11-24, v1.0, URL 1999-11-24).

8 G. Smith, *Interpreting the Prophetic Books* (ed. D. Howard Jr; Grand Rapids, MI: Kregel Academic, 2012), p. 74.

9 M. Henry, 'Joel Chapter One', https://www.biblegateway.com/resources/matthew-henry/Joel.1.1-Joel.1.20 (accessed 2 August 2020).

10 R.B. Chisholm, Jr, 'Joel', in *The Bible Knowledge Commentary (Old Testament)* (ed. John F. Walvoord and Roy B. Zuck; Wheaton, IL.: Victor Books, 1985), p. 1412.

11 Jonathan Graf, *Restored Power: Becoming a Praying Church One Tweak at a Time* (California, CA: PrayerShop Fellowship, 2016).

12 Zeph. 2:1–3.

13 Isa. 55:6,7.

14 Jer. 3:12,13.

15 B. Beach, K. Clay and M.H. Saavedra, 'The 1918 Influenza Pandemic and Its Lessons for COVID-19',National Bureau of Economic Research Working Paper Series, 2020, (w27673), https://www.nber.org/papers/w27673 (accessed 17 September 2020).

## 9 Obadiah Remember Who God Is

[1] K. Sawrey, *The Infographic Bible* (London: William Collins, 2018), p. 121.

[2] 1 Kgs 18:4.

[3] 2 Kgs 8:20–22; 2 Chr. 21:8–10.

[4] Ps. 137.

[5] J.C. Dykehouse, 'An Historical Reconstruction of Edomite Treaty Betrayal in the Sixth Century B.C.E. Based on Biblical, Epigraphic, and Archaeological Data', *ProQuest*, 2008, p. 11, https://baylor-ir.tdl.org/handle/2104/5159 (accessed 7 September 2020).

[6] E. Ben Zvi, *A Historical-Critical Study of the Book of Obadiah* (Berlin: Walter de Gruyter, 1996), pp. 104–6.

[7] Ben Zvi, *A Historical-Critical Study of the Book of Obadiah*, pp. 104–6.

[8] W.P. Brown, *Obadiah through Malachi* (Louisville, KY: Westminster John Knox Press, 1996), p. 7.

[9] Brown, *Obadiah through Malachi*, pp. 10–26.

[10] Brown, *Obadiah through Malachi*, p. 1.

[11] Prof. Itzhaq Beit-Arieh, 'Edomites Advance into Judah', *Biblical Archaeology Review* (1996), https://www.baslibrary.org/biblical-archaeology-review/22/6/4 (accessed 3 August 2020).

[12] Liat Kornowski, 'Celebrity Tour Riders: Stars' Most Bizarre Requests On Tour, From Kittens To Hookers To Flowers', https://www.huffingtonpost.co.uk/entry/celebrity-tour-riders (accessed 2 August 2020).

[13] https://www.gigwise.com/news/79335/ (accessed 17 September 2020).

[14] 2 Cor. 5:10.

## 10 Zechariah A Call for Hope in a Hopeless Time

[1] C. Meyers and E. Meyers, *Haggai, Zechariah 1–8 (The Anchor Bible)* (Garden City, NY: Doubleday and Company Inc., 1987), p. 183.

2   S. Grigor, *The Making of the Georgian Nation* (Bloomington, IN: Indiana University Press, 1994).

3   United Nations Press Release 14 October 1971 (SG/SM/1553/HQ263), https://www.google.com/url?sa=t&rct=j&q=&esrc=s&source=web&cd=&ved=2ahUKEwjXwPuE3NTrAhXG-aQKHXJgA9UQFjAAegQIBBAB&url=https%3A%2F%2Fsearch.archives.un.org%2Fuploads%2Fr%2Funited-nations-archives%2F6%2F0%2Fe%2F60e01378f4efade1353c642dc378bc5544138ce0ce2f3f4cab3a7ad37905a49a%2FS-0882-0002-02-00001.pdf&usg=AOvVaw2A6YzKuo654cOmxrJURGf_ (accessed 28 August 2020).

4   C. Sinclair, *The Hitch-Hiker's Guide to the Bible* (Oxford: Monarch Books, 2008).

5   S. Sabz, 'Literal or Symbolic? Apocalyptic Symbols Revealed' (2017), https://scienceandbibleresearch.com/literal-or-symbolic-apocalyptic-symbols-revealed.html (accessed 7 September 2020).

6   Name and details disguised.

## 11 Haggai   A Call for Strength

1   Ezra 2:64,65.

2   Ezra 6:1–12.

3   See Jer. 29:10-14 as an example of God's promise to lead His people out of exile.

4   Ezra 1:1–4; Neh. 2:1–9.

5   It is recommended that you read the book of Esther.

6   The Startup Strategy, https://inspire99.com/either-you-run-the-day-or-the-day-runs-you-jim-rohn/ (accessed 7 September 2020).

7   S. Claiborne, J. Wilson-Hartgrove and E. Okoro, *Common Prayer: A Liturgy for Ordinary Radicals* (Grand Rapids, MI: Zondervan, 2010), p. 20.

## 12  Malachi    A Message of Hope

[1]  R.J. Coggins, *Haggai, Zechariah, Malachi* (Edinburgh: A&C Black, 1987), p. 20.
[2]  G. Smith, *Interpreting the Prophetic Books* (ed. D. Howard Jr; Grand Rapids, MI: Kregel Academic, 2012).
[3]  See Haggai and Zechariah.
[4]  Ezra 2:64,65.

### The Final Word

[1]  WHO Director-General's opening remarks at the media briefing on COVID-19 – 11 March 2020, https://www.who.int/dg/speeches/detail/who-director-general-s-opening-remarks-at-the-media-briefing-on-covid-19-11-march-2020 (accessed 17 September 2020).
[2]  G. Garrison, 'What Clergy Said When Influenza Closed Churches in 1918', https://www.al.com/coronavirus/2020/04/what-clergy-said-when-influenza-closed-churches-in-1918.html (accessed 2 August 2020).
[3]  J. Welby, 'Prayer is a Partnership with God', https://www.archbishopofcanterbury.org/prayer-partnership-god (accessed 7 September 2020).
[4]  P. Grieg, *How to Pray* (London: Hodder & Stoughton, 2019).
[5]  C. Collins, 'More Brits Turning to Prayer During COVID-19 Lockdown', https://cruxnow.com/church-in-uk-and-ireland/2020/05/more-brits-turning-to-prayer-during-covid-19-lockdown/ (accessed 2 August 2020).
[6]  H. Sherwood, 'Religion. British Public Turn to Prayer as One in Four Tune in to Religious Services,' https://www.theguardian.com/world/2020/may/03/british-public-turn-to-prayer-as-one-in-four-tune-in-to-religious-services (accessed 2 August 2020).

7   G. Garrison, 'What Clergy Said When Influenza Closed Churches in 1918', https://www.msn.com/en-us/news/us/what-clergy-said-when-influenza-closed-churches-in-1918/ar-BB12NfVA (accessed 7 September 2020).

8   Garrison, 'What Clergy Said When Influenza Closed Churches in 1918', ibid.

## Appendix

1   Used and edited with permission.

**A–Z of Prayer**

*Building strong foundations for
daily conversations with God*

*Matthew Porter*

*A–Z of Prayer* is an accessible introduction that gives practical
guidance on how to develop a meaningful prayer life. It presents
twenty-six aspects of prayer to help you grow in your
relationship with God, explore new devotional styles and
deepen your daily conversations with God.

Each topic has a few pages of introduction and insight, an
action section for reflection and application and a prayer
to help put the action point into practice. There are also
references to allow further study.

978-1-78893-062-8

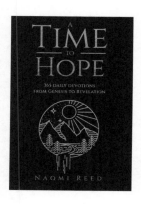

**A Time to Hope**

*365 Daily devotions from
Genesis to Revelation*

*Naomi Reed*

Many of us have favourite Bible verses that we draw comfort from, but we don't always know their context or understand how they fit into the main story arc of the Bible.

Tracing the big picture of God's story through the key themes and events from Genesis to Revelation allows us to see the abundant riches in God's Word. As you read the unfolding story day by day, you can encounter God in all his glorious holiness and faithfulness.

If you have ever struggled to read the Bible from cover to cover, then this devotional will help you find a way in to God's big story and help you fall in love with Jesus all over again.

978-1-78893-144-1

**Authentic**

We trust you enjoyed reading this book
from Authentic. If you want to be
informed of any new titles from this author
and other releases you can sign up to the
Authentic newsletter by scanning below:

Online:
authenticmedia.co.uk

Follow us: